Alice Mabel Bacon

A Japanese Interior

Alice Mabel Bacon

A Japanese Interior

ISBN/EAN: 9783337171087

Printed in Europe, USA, Canada, Australia, Japan

Cover: Foto ©ninafisch / pixelio.de

More available books at **www.hansebooks.com**

A JAPANESE INTERIOR

BY

ALICE MABEL BACON
AUTHOR OF "JAPANESE GIRLS AND WOMEN"

BOSTON AND NEW YORK
HOUGHTON, MIFFLIN AND COMPANY
The Riverside Press, Cambridge
1893

Copyright, 1893,
By ALICE MABEL BACON.

All rights reserved.

The Riverside Press, Cambridge, Mass., U. S. A.
Electrotyped and Printed by H. O. Houghton & Co.

To

MY BROTHERS AND SISTERS

FOR WHOM THESE LETTERS WERE ORIGINALLY WRITTEN,

THIS PRINTED VOLUME

IS AFFECTIONATELY INSCRIBED.

PREFACE.

The letters presented to the public in this book were written during an experience of life in Japan somewhat different from that of the average foreign resident in the East. The author's call to the Orient came to her from one of the most conservative and anti-foreign of the Tōkyō schools, — a school for noble girls, under the management of the Imperial Household Department. The invitation was sent to her through a Japanese friend, who had been the teacher of English in the school since its foundation, for no foreigner's recommendation would have had much weight with the conservative and cultivated Japanese in charge of the institution. Work in such a school naturally brings a teacher into close contact with the most refined and cultivated of Japanese women, and cannot fail to give to those who perform it a new sympathy with a class usually but little understood.

Upon my arrival in Tōkyō in June, 1888, I found myself greeted by Japanese friends, known long and intimately in America, but from whom I had been separated for years. Their friendship had, however, stood well the strain of the long separation both by time and space. In all that great city I had no acquaintance of my own race and language, but my Japanese friends so cared for me and surrounded me by their kindness, that instead of missing the society of my own people, I found its absence a positive advantage, in that it threw me entirely upon congenial and interesting Japanese friends for that social intercourse necessary for all civilized beings.

Journeys over the beaten tracks of tourist travel during the summer of 1888 brought me in contact with many charming and interesting American and English people, acquaintances kept up during my stay in Japan; but my home and life while in Tōkyō was among the Japanese, the excursions made into the foreign world forming merely agreeable and unusual incidents.

My home in Tōkyō was a house — half Japanese and half foreign — on a little hill in the Kōjimachi district, the central district of the city. Above our house on the hill ran a great business street, where the influence of foreign ideas was as yet but little felt, and along which many of our most interesting walks were taken. A short walk in another direction led past the old-fashioned palace of Prince Fushimi, over a great moat, and up to the gates of the Akasaka Palace, the residence of the Emperor until the year 1889. Out from this palace gate the Empress, attended by her ladies, used to walk to visit her pet institution, the Peeresses' School, so near did it stand to the palace inclosure. At about the same distance on the other side of us stood the fine modern residence of Prince Kitashirakawa, and a little further prolongation of the walk carried one into the region occupied by the foreign legations and the official residences of the Cabinet Ministers, and up to the moat that encircles the heart of the city, — the ancient castle of the Shōgun, within whose mighty ramparts stands the new Imperial Palace.

Within our house, my part, built as the Japanese are pleased to call it in "foreign style," — that is, with two stories, glass windows, swing doors, and a hole in the wall for the stovepipe to go through, — contained two rooms and a front entry, and was furnished after the manner common to American houses. This was connected with the purely Japanese part of the mansion by the engawa, a polished-wood-floored piazza, roofed by the overhanging eaves, and shut in at night by the solid sliding shutters or amado, so as to form a corridor along the garden side of the house.

The front was provided with two entrances, — one into the foreign rooms, within which shoes might come, and one into the Japanese rooms by means of a little vestibule with low, latticed gate, where clogs must be laid aside before stepping upon the soft, white mats which form, not floor-covering only, but chairs, tables, and spring mattresses as well in a Japanese home. My paper-walled dining-room, my only Japanese room, projected from the front of the house between these two entrances, and from it, as I took my solitary meals in "foreign style," accompanied by all the formalities of table, chairs, and knives and forks, I could hear the cheerful bustle that seemed always to hover about the Japanese entrance. Here was the place for the putting on of shoes, as in cumbersome foreign dress our family took their early start for school. At this place bows and saio naras were exchanged on the part of all in the house whenever one member of the family went away on so much as a shopping expedition; here, too, sounded the cheerful "O kaeri," that announced the return of one of the occupants of the house, the breathless "O kyaku" shouted by the kurumaya of the coming guest so soon as he was within the gate, or the deprecating "Go men nasai," with which an applicant for admission made known his presence.

One kitchen sufficed for our family, but two cooks and two stoves were necessary for our double household. My own cook, upon a stove of foreign manufacture, prepared my food after the foreign manner, while the little gozen taki with her Japanese stove, aided by numerous shichi rin, did the cooking for the rest of the family. Outside of the kitchen were the servants' quarters, and near the back gate stood a small stable with a three-mat room, for the accommodation of the groom and his family.

Toward the garden, the house formed two sides of a square, along which ran the engawa connecting foreign and Japanese buildings. A step out of my long window and down this shining piazza brought me into the very heart of a Japanese home. Here the family gathered about the hibachi of a cold day or in the winter evenings. Here they sat on the floor and sewed, constructing kimono, obi, haori, and other graceful and dainty garments with paper thimble, a long needle upon which the cloth is run, and an endless thread, cut off from the reel only when the seam is finished. Here they told stories, exchanged ideas, studied lessons, and accorded warmest welcome at all times to the foreigner attracted thither by the life and interest that seemed always about the rooms.

On sunny days, the little garden, with its pine-tree, its cherry and plum trees, its camelia hedge, its stone lantern, and its perennial succession of flowers, was our common playground. Here we all laughed together over my first attempts with Japanese clogs and the Japanese language; here my American collie chased their tailless Japanese cat, to the never-failing amusement of all parties concerned; here was the centre, perhaps, of our home life in all but the worst weather. Was I lonely? Into the garden I went, and straightway from some room of the Japanese house a bright-eyed little friend would make her way out to join me, and soon another, and then another would step down from the engawa into her waiting clogs, and then a game, or a run, or a new flower, or something of absorbing interest would engross us all.

Our household was composed entirely of women, — three of us teachers in the Peeresses' School, three pupils in the same institution, and two young girls living in the family for the sake of the culture, especially in English, to be derived from such society. These, with the servants needed for the establishment, my dog, and the two cats, made up a congenial company.

Such were the surroundings amid which most of these letters were written. Whatever views they may give of Japanese life were obtained from the Japanese side, and from the side of the Japanese woman, although undoubtedly much affected by passing through the medium of an American mind. The letters do not lay claim to deep research or wide knowledge of all subjects touched upon by them. They are simply a daily chronicle of events, sights, and impressions. They have the character of the product of a photographic camera rather than of an artist's brush. Whatever theories are advanced are put forward as the material from which thought may be made, and not as the result of mature deliberation. The book is more a picture of the life of one foreigner among the Japanese, and a record of her thoughts about their civilization and her own, than it is an authority on Japan in general, or on any particular phase of life there.

To all my Japanese friends my thanks are due for whatever I have seen or known or enjoyed in their country, and if through lack of tact or wisdom or literary skill anything has found a place in this volume that their clearer judgment would have left unpublished, pardon is asked now for all offenses. My thought throughout the work of editing these letters has been to preserve, so far as possible, without violating confidence, or that sweet seclusion that is so characteristic a feature of Japanese home life, the little touches of nature that make the whole world kin, and bring into one human brotherhood all races under heaven.

CONTENTS.

I.

Tōkyō, September 5 to 26.

Going to Housekeeping. — An Evening Walk. — Fireworks and Rochester Lamps. — A Foreign Restaurant. — Shopping at the Kwan-ko-ba. — Settling Accounts. — Introduction to the Peeresses. — School Routine. — Story of Boy and Crab. — Jinrikisha Riding. — The Climate 1

II.

October 1 to 15.

A Sunday Visit. — "Bōt' Chan." — Preparations for a Horse. — The Peeresses' English Society. — Tōkyō from a Horse's Back. — English as a Dead Language. — Dawn. — A Sunday-School Class. — Mr. Kozaki. — Difficulties with the Kana. — Bruce and the Bettō. — Lecture on Bandai San. — Prince Haru. — Difficulties in Church-Going. — A Japanese Meal 19

III.

October 21 to November 4.

Mr. Kozaki's Church. — Introduction to Bible Class. — Reception Days. — A Hibachi. — Two Old

Ladies. — My Paper Dining-Room. — Funeral Fashions. — An Official Funeral. — Simplicity of Japanese Living. — Posthumous Titles. — The Emperor's Birthday 33

IV.

November 12 to 14.

A Nō Performance. — Death of Prince Aki. — Dango Zaka 59

V.

November 25 to December 18.

A Ball at the Rokumei-kwan. — A Tōkyō Story. — Bōt' Chan's Studies in Physiognomy. — Thanksgiving and Turkey. — Christmas Carols. — Fuji-Yama. — The New Palace. — Tōkyō Moats. — Bowing to Prince Haru 77

VI.

December 27 to January 6.

Christmas Preparations. — Hanging Stockings. — English Service. — A Church Festival. — New Year's Decorations. — New Year's Eve on Ginza. — A Street Fight. — New Year's Day. — Street Performers. — An Earthquake. — Kurumayas in Cold Weather 91

VII.

January 13 to 30.

Discharging a Groom. — The New Kurumaya. — The Emperor's Moving-Day. — A New Year's Lunch.

— Buying a Kuruma. — A New Horse. — The Japanese Language. — The Promulgation of the Constitution. — Tombs of the Loyal Rōnin . . . 110

VIII.

FEBRUARY 12 TO 20.

The Promulgation Festival. — Morning Scenes on Kojimachi. — Exercises at the School. — Imperial Progress through Tōkyō Streets. — Evening Rides and Street Sights. — Rice and Eels. — Mingling with the Holiday Crowd. — Murder of Viscount Mori. — Viscount Mori's Funeral. — Religious Liberty under the Constitution. — Another Earthquake 129

IX.

MARCH 1 TO 9.

The Wily Bettō. — Yasaku's Domestic Affairs. — Marriage and Divorce. — Developments in Regard to the Mori Murder. — Letters from Nishino to his Family. — A Spring Jaunt. — Toy Collecting . . 147

X.

MARCH 21 TO 31.

A Sad Holiday. — Japanese Mourning Customs. — A Shintō Funeral. — An Earthquake. — Yasaku's Wedding. — Questions on John's Gospel 161

XI.

APRIL 6 TO 14.

A Country Walk. — Feast of Dolls at a Daimiō's Yashiki. — Picnic at Mito Yashiki. — A Day at the Theatre. — Japanese Acting 174

XII.

APRIL 19 TO MAY 2.

The Empress' Visit. — Presentation to the Empress. — A Buddhist Funeral. — A Garden Party. — Questions on John's Gospel 189

XIII.

MAY 8 TO JUNE 22.

Summer Weather. — A Matsuri. — Early School. — Perry Expedition Reports. — Bible Class of School-Girls. — Fighting Fleas. — Japanese Servants. — The New School-Building. — The Peeresses' Literary Society. — A Speech by Mr. Knapp. — Scandal 204

XIV.

JUNE 29 TO JULY 24.

School-Building Trouble settled. — A Japanese Baby. — Shopping. — Japanese Taste. — Facts and Theories. — Calls from Drs. Brooks and McVickar. — Packing in Wet Weather. — Farewell Presents. — Graduating Exercises. — Near View of the Empress. — Correcting Proof under Difficulties 223

XV.

HIYÉI ZAN, JULY 31, TO NUMADZU, AUGUST 28.

View from Hiyéi Zan. — The Mission Camp. — Last Days in Tōkyō. — Voyage to Kobé. — From

Kobé to Hiyéi. — Historical Interest of Hiyéi. — Pleasant Weather and Walks. — A Young Buddhist. — Some Effects of the Summer Camp. — Benkei's Relics. — The "Hiyéi Zan Hornet." — Shopping in Kiōtō. — The River at Night. — Illumination of the Mountains. — A Snake Story. — Traveling in Japanese Style. — Start in a Typhoon. — Nagoya. — A Wayside Inn. — Okazaki. — Weak Kurumayas. — An Unpleasant Hotel. Okitsu. — End of the Journey. — Numadzu. — Children's Visits. — Slow Freight. — Plans for Home. 239

A JAPANESE INTERIOR.

CHAPTER I.

SEPTEMBER 5 TO 26.

Going to Housekeeping. — An Evening Walk. — Fireworks and Rochester Lamps. — A Foreign Restaurant. — Shopping at the Kwan-ko-ba. — Settling Accounts. — Introduction to the Peeresses. — School Routine. — Story of Boy and Crab. — Jinrikisha Riding. — The Climate.

Kioi Cho, Tōkyō,
Wednesday, September 5, 1888.

I CAME down from Nikkō on Monday, alone. My new cook met me, and brought me and the few worldly goods I had with me safely up to my new house. He seems anxious to do what I want and willing to turn his hand to anything, but as he does not know any English and I know very little Japanese, it is sometimes hard for him to grasp my idea. Miné has to do a good deal of work at present as an interpreter, but I hope soon to be able to give orders myself to my servants in their own language.

I find that the business of getting settled in Japan involves a good deal of sitting still and waiting for people to do things. Just now, I am having an enforced rest, for my cook has gone off, leaving word that he is sick. Miné is away, so that I cannot do some shopping that I wish to; all my trunks are unpacked and my clothes put away, and there is absolutely nothing that I can do, in spite of the fact that there is a great deal to be accomplished.

Last evening, Miné and her train of girls who live in the house took me out to walk and do some errands. We walked along a broad street with lighted shops on both sides, along which a great concourse of people were moving up and down, with no end in view, I imagine, except to enjoy the coolness of the evening after an excessively hot day. Here and there on mats laid on the ground, or in little booths, were spread out the wares of some enterprising peddler, — sometimes a stock of fruit, sometimes a great display of wooden ware, sometimes a traveling restaurant, with curious concoctions of rice, fish, seaweed, etc., to tempt the appetite of the hungry pedestrian. One booth was filled with minute cages, from which proceeded a tremendous chirping, produced by various kinds of singing insects, — crickets, katydids, grasshoppers, etc. All up and down the street there was a glare of small kerosene torches, like those used in torchlight processions at home, only smaller. These served to light each dealer's display pretty well. At one place where we stopped to inquire the price of melons, Bruce caught sight of a cat prowling about, and made a rush at it with such good effect that the cat sprang into the middle of our fruit vender's stock-in-trade, hitting one of his torches and throwing it over. Luckily, watermelons are not inflammable, so no harm was done, though the torch lay on its side for some time, burning merrily, before it was picked up. After this adventure, Bruce walked along ignominiously at the end of a strap during the remainder of our expedition. Whenever we stopped to make a purchase, a crowd gathered and watched our doings most intently. Apparently, a foreign lady with a dog shopping at that time of night is not a common sight in this part of the city, and we began to feel very much like a traveling show as audience after audience gathered around us, to disperse again when we moved on.

When we returned from our walk, I went into Miné's part of the house, and we had a queer little feast. First Miné handed around some beans, roasted in a corn-popper as we do chestnuts. They were very nice, except that after a while they seemed rather choky. Then I offered the company some candy that I had bought at one of the booths, a kind of jelly, as clear as glass, coated with sugar. Then we topped off with a glass of raspberry vinegar all around. This proved to be an entire novelty to Miné's Japanese friends, and they were delighted with it. To end our exciting evening, the girls set off some fireworks. First they tried some of the little Japanese parlor fireworks that we see in America, and these were very pretty and went off successfully. Then one of the girls lighted something of the rocket or Roman candle species, that fired balls from a stick set in the ground. But this was rather a failure, for Bruce decided that it was a dangerous weapon, and as soon as it began to go he made a rush at it and bit the lighted end off, setting the hair on his chin and around his neck in a blaze, but entirely discouraging the rocket. He then came back, singed but happy, and quite sure that he had rescued us from a great danger. After this excitement, the whole family came with me to my parlor, to see the new Rochester lamp which I had just had hung. They were much impressed by the magnificent light that it gave, and Miné's cousin, a dear little sweet-faced widow, the chaperon of our establishment, poetically remarked that my lamp was like the sun, and theirs was like a little star.

September 7.

You would be amused to see the manner in which I am greeted at the little restaurant where Bruce and I are now taking our dinners. My affairs are so far settled that my cook is able to achieve a simple breakfast in the house, but we have not attempted dinner, so I take it every evening at the little foreign restaurant around the corner. I tie Bruce in the yard before I go in, and this stop gives time for the whole force of the house to assemble in the entry, where they draw up in line, and salute me as I pass with the lowest and most graceful of bows. The tail end of the line consists of two small boys, just the same size and dressed exactly alike, who look as if they could not be more than ten years old, they are so small and have such baby faces, but they make as elaborate and beautiful bows as if they were dancing-masters.

September 8.

Yesterday I made a visit to the Kwan-ko-ba at Shiba to buy the china necessary for my housekeeping. This big bazaar is a very interesting place, because there you can find under one roof an epitome of everything that Japan makes or wants, to wear or to use about the house. The Shiba Kwan-ko-ba is the largest in Tōkyō, and has a great many different stalls kept by independent tradesmen. The advantage of the place to inexperienced persons like myself is that everything has its price fixed and plainly marked upon it according to its quality, so that there is no danger of being overcharged or cheated. Here I bought, for the moderate sum of ten yen, all the china that I can use at my small table, and all pretty and dainty in design and finish, so that I am now ready to begin my housekeeping, if I can make my cook understand that I wish him to order the necessary supplies from the grocer.

September 10.

To-night I had my first settling of accounts with my cook, a function that had to be conducted largely with the aid of a dictionary. My man squatted on the floor in front of me, and took out from the folds of his gown a queer little account-book, in which he had written some hieroglyphics that he found a good deal of difficulty in deciphering. With many suckings in of the breath, he would enunciate as clearly and loudly as possible the Japanese word for the thing purchased, and if I did not know what it was, I had to look it up in the dictionary before we could go farther. Then came the price in Japanese, which after my summer of shopping and traveling presented no difficulties to me, and then both purchase and price must be transferred to my account-book. We spent a long time over one word, which he pronounced as if it were spelled " tabu," so I looked it up in my dictionary, and was in despair when I could find no such word, until suddenly it came over me that he was trying to say "tub." What with his Japonicized English and my Anglicized Japanese we find it hard to understand each other, but I hope that soon the spur of necessity will so far improve my Japanese as to remove these little difficulties.

September 17.

To-day I have been over to the school for the first time in my official capacity, and have seen and been introduced to my classes and my superiors, and to-morrow I begin work. Miné introduced me to Mrs. Shimoda, the lady principal, who does not speak any English, so we were obliged to exchange polite speeches through the medium of Miné's interpretation. Then I was taken to a little room, where I was shown a desk in which I can keep whatever books, stationery, etc., I may wish to have at the school, and at which I can sit between classes. Every teacher has such a desk, and it seems a very convenient arrangement. Here I was left to meditate until called for, but the time did not seem long, for I was busy watching the other teachers in the room and conversing with Miss H., the only foreigner beside myself in the employ of the school. When Miné came back, she offered to take me about and introduce me to my classes. So we went from room to room, and as Miné announced my name to the group of orderly little peeresses seated in each room, the children bowed most reverentially and gracefully. Then I bowed, as well as I know how, though I think that bowing is a lost art in America. This ceremony ended, Miné would speak a few words in Japanese to the class, and so give me time to look over my future pupils. I was introduced to five classes after this manner, and then my work for the morning was over, so I went back to my desk, while Miné went on to salute her own classes.

After a while it was announced that all the teachers and pupils were to assemble in the gymnasium, there to be addressed by the principal, an elderly and scholarly gentleman of the old school, but one who speaks not a word of English. We went down to the gymnasium, which is connected with the main school building by a covered walk, and met all the girls on their way thither, each class under the leadership of a teacher. I saw one roguish little face laughing at me from among the crowd, and recognized one of Yuki's little daughters, who has to-day taken her first plunge into school life. She seemed to be enjoying her morning's experience, and fairly danced herself out of line when she found that I had recognized her. When we finally reached the gymnasium, we found it filled with girls arranged in line according to size, with all the smallest ones in front. When I saw them, my thoughts could not but fly back to Hampton, and contrast our poor little pickaninnies there with these little peeresses. But they are alike in one way, and that is that their lives are more or less stunted and cramped by the circumstances of their birth, the pickaninnies by poverty and the disabilities of their low social position, the peeresses by the rigid restraints and formalities that accompany their rank.

Very pretty children these little peeresses are, in spite of the ugly foreign dress into which the school requirements force them. Their mothers have undoubtedly tried hard to have them well dressed for the first day of school, but most of the dresses have evidently been chosen and made by people not in the least familiar with any style of European garment, and are now worn in such a way as to make the children look, so far as clothes go, like the veriest clodhoppers, instead of the descendants of perhaps the oldest aristocracy in the world. The shoes and stockings especially show the parent's ignorance of the niceties of foreign dress, for the stockings are of the coarsest wool in the gaudiest of colored stripes, making the slender well-shaped legs look heavy and shapeless, and the shoes are the roughest calfskin, in many cases much too large for the small feet. But there the children stand in their queer clothes, all silent and orderly, though no one is keeping order, and the teachers are bustling about, talking among themselves. Any company of American children would be uncontrollable if kept standing so long with nothing to do, but these children are too well mannered to be noisy in the presence of their elders, and so they stand like statues and wait. After a while the principal comes forward and bows, and all the children bend themselves nearly double in return; then he makes a very short speech and bows again, and once more the whole three hundred and fifty bow simultaneously. Then Mrs. Shimoda comes to the front and bows, and again the little audience bows in response. It is a very pretty custom, and I do not see why, when a speaker bows to his audience, the audience should not return the compliment. It seems quite the natural and polite thing to do, but is a little surprising at first sight. Mrs. Shimoda makes a short speech, and then one of the directors speaks, and after that the children are marshaled out again by their teachers. That is the end of the morning's exercises, and Miné and I only wait to draw our text-books from the school library, before going home.

I have been looking over my text-books since I came back, among others an American "Universal History," in which I find the following statement: "The only historic race is the Caucasian, the others having done little worth recording." It seems to me that this will be a very interesting piece of news to a class of Japanese girls who are already quite familiar with the wonderfully stirring and heroic history of their own country. I asked Miné what she thought they would say to that, and she replied that she should think they would say that the book was written by a Caucasian. I have decided to skip the introduction which contains this statement, so as to avoid showing to my pupils the self-conceit of my own race.

September 20.

My work has now fairly begun, and while impressions are fresh I will write them down, so that you may know how the peeresses strike me on first acquaintance. The first thing that one notices after American schools is the absolute absence of discipline, or of any necessity for it. The pupils are all so perfectly lady-like that politeness restrains them from doing anything that is not exactly what their teachers or superiors would wish them to do. There is no noise in the corridors, no whispering in the classes, nothing but the most perfect attention to what the teacher says, and the most earnest desire to be careful and thoughtful always of the feelings of others, especially of the teachers. Miné says that in addition to this there is in the Peeresses' School a most remarkably high sense of honor, so that the teacher can be quite sure that her pupils will never be guilty of cheating, or shamming, or trying to improve their standing by any false methods. Though the old nobility may be run out physically and mentally, their sense of honor is something wonderful, and the feeling of *noblesse oblige* is so strong that they scorn all petty meannesses as something not in keeping with their rank. It is very interesting to me, in reading over the names on my class lists, to notice that some of them were famous in Japanese history long before Columbus discovered America. Somehow the centuries of honor in which the families have been held have told upon the daughters, and they are ladies in the finest sense of that much-abused word, even when dressed in such shapeless and dowdy clothes that a beggar woman in America would turn up her nose at them.

And now, perhaps, you would be interested to hear a little of the daily school routine. When I go over in the morning, my first duty is to register my name in the record of attendance. This I do with a little seal upon which my name is inscribed in Japanese, for the seal in Japan is used instead of the autograph signature in America. I have just learned to seal my name right side up, and to recognize it when it is written in Japanese, and I regard this as a great advancement over my former state of ignorance. Having thus recorded myself as present, I go to my desk, and there await the ringing of the bell that calls the girls in from the playground and the teachers to meet their classes. When the bell rings, I go to my recitation room, and there, ranged in line outside of the door, is my class awaiting me. I bow as low as I can, the pupils bow still lower, and then go into the room. They take their places quietly and stand; I bow from my place at the teacher's desk, again the girls bow, and take their seats, and for fifty minutes we labor with the intricacies of the English language. The signal for the close of the lesson is given by a man who walks through the corridors clapping a pair of wooden clappers. When I hear that sound, I finish the lesson, and bow to the class, who all bow, rise, and marching quietly out of the door range themselves in order and wait for me. I walk out, bow to them once more, they make a farewell obeisance, and quietly disperse for the ten-minute recess that comes at the end of each fifty-minute recitation. The whole thing is very pretty, and I am charmed with this manner of calling to order and dismissing classes. It might have a civilizing effect, if introduced into American schools.

September 26.

I am going to copy into this letter a funny little bit of translation that was handed me as a school exercise a day or two ago. The young lady who did it must have translated it word for word from the Japanese, using the first word that she found in the dictionary, and the result is a little obscure at times.

The Story of Boy and Crab.

Some boy was playing at river bank and saw a crab going away. Then the boy call back the crab and said this track is straight but why you go sideways? The crab angry and said I am ashame, not straight hard, not ashame, shape is transverse because my natural constitution is transverse, so I go transverse, but your natural constitution is length, so you must go at length. You do not go transverse in a cross road. When you forget your natural constitution and do my imitation, I hand up my nail and cut your body and go looking askent and again going away.

Yesterday, Miné and I had a most exciting jinrikisha ride. Our men were very strong and fast, and seemed to be as fresh as two colts just feeling their oats. They raced with each other most of the time while we were out, and it seemed to me a good deal like riding a frisky horse with no bridle. They ran so fast through the business streets that my heart was in my mouth most of the way for fear they would run us into something, or upset us in switching suddenly around a corner. My man almost ran over a child, in fact, the hub of the wheel struck the child on the knee, and a minute or two afterward he came within a hair's breadth of running into the kuruma of an elderly Japanese gentleman who was just ahead of us in the road. The worst of this kind of thing is that, while you have no control whatever over your man, you cannot help feeling responsible for his carelessness.

The weather has only just become so cool that I am not perfectly comfortable in the thinnest kind of a white dress, but yesterday I was actually frozen out of it, and I suppose I may put my thin dresses away now until next summer. I should say, from my brief experience of this climate, that it is much more to be depended upon than our own, and not subject to the sudden and violent changes that characterize all the climates I have yet tried in America. After the warm weather has once begun here, one could go away into the country and stay for two months without a particle of woolen clothing, and never be chilly a moment. There is none of that one day summer and the next day winter that we have to provide for at home.

CHAPTER II.

OCTOBER 1 TO 15.

A Sunday Visit. — "Bōt' Chan." — Preparations for a Horse. — The Peeresses' English Society. — Tōkyō from a Horse's Back. — English as a Dead Language. — Dawn. — A Sunday-School Class. — Mr. Kozaki. — Difficulties with the Kana. — Bruce and the Bettō. — Lecture on Bandai San. — Prince Haru. — Difficulties in Church-Going. — A Japanese Meal.

Monday, October 1, 1888.

SUNDAY afternoon, I went out to a suburb of Tōkyō, where Yuki's husband has been putting up a fine new foreign house. It was designed by a German architect here, and is different from most of the foreign houses in the city in being comfortable and well built, and looking quite like some of our pleasant American homes. There is a little farm about the house, with tea-plants, strawberry-vines, sweet potatoes, and various other fruits and vegetables growing finely. There are beautiful chestnut-trees, too, on which large nuts, like the Spanish chestnuts, are just ripening. When I reached the house, which is as yet not quite finished, I was much puzzled as to how I was to get in, and was wandering about searching for traces of the party that I knew to be gathered there, when Yuki's eldest daughter came out of the last door that I should ever have thought of entering, and conducted me up flight after flight of stairs to the very top of the house. Here a room had been finished off, and furnished with Japanese mats. Quite a company was assembled there, many of them English-speaking Japanese and friends or acquaintances of mine. All were seated upon the floor in the comfortable Japanese fashion, but a pile of cushions was made for me out of respect for my stiff foreign joints. A curious kind of lunch was spread out on the floor, consisting of sweet potatoes (always eaten here between meals, never as a vegetable with meals), a kind of root which has a leaf something like a calla, and boiled, to be eaten with salt, and fruit of various kinds. There were grapes, fresh figs, pomegranates, persimmons, and the queer, hard Japanese pears that look like russet apples, and taste like some kind of medicine when they have any flavor at all, which is not often. There was of course the inevitable tea, of which I have now grown quite fond. When we had nibbled in a desultory way at this repast, Yuki took me out to show me the place. We went first over the house, her husband going with us, and beaming graciously at my approval of the arrangements, for this house is one of his hobbies, and he takes the utmost delight in every window-fastening and door-knob. Then we went out for a look at the grounds; first to the tennis lawn, where about a dozen children were having a frolic. They formed a picturesque group in their pretty Japanese clothes, and seemed to be having a delightful and harmonious time. When we had watched the children for a while, we made a tour of the grounds, "Bōt' chan" going with us, and conducting himself in a most serious and dignified manner, until finally, as the shortness of his legs somewhat hindered our progress, his mother confided him to the care of his valet. He is a fine, sturdy boy, with curly black hair cut very short, a stately way of holding his head, and a somewhat serious cast of countenance. His tastes are warlike and equestrian, and he has a white

Arabian horse on which he rides with the assistance of the groom, though he is not yet three years old. He has also a beautiful, small sword, of the finest Japanese steel, but he despises this because it is not large enough, and wants his father's.

By the time we had finished our tour, the guests were preparing to depart, so I went too, and trotted gayly home in my jinrikisha with my favorite fast man. Bruce greatly delighted my kurumaya by defeating utterly a dog of about twice his size, who came up and attacked him from behind as he was following the jinrikisha. The man turned around in the shafts and delivered quite a harangue, in which I could catch only the word "inu," but concluded that it was in commendation of Bruce's pluck, as he smiled most approvingly upon him.

October 5.

To-day has been quite exciting to me and my household, for a horse has come in for trial, and I have been seeing to having him installed in the stable, and paying the bills for the various mysterious things that a Japanese groom regards as indispensable. I am to try the beast to-morrow, and hope that he will be what I want, as it would be very pleasant to be able to settle the horse question without further trouble. Horses here are put into their stalls wrong end foremost, so that I never go into the stable without thinking of the nursery rhyme, —

"See! See! What shall I see?
A horse's head where its tail should be."

The author of the couplet must have visited Japan.

Miné and I are to have our girls here Saturday night for an English evening. It is one of the few festivities that the poor girls are allowed to go to, as their rank is too high to permit them to enjoy themselves like common folks. The girls of the highest rank are not, as a rule, permitted even to enter the houses of the samurai class, but because we are their teachers they can come to us, although they could not go anywhere else. Teachers are held in great esteem here, and the profession is a most honorable one, so that even if you are teaching the future Emperor, you are for the time being his superior.

October 6.

I have had my first ride this afternoon, and enjoyed it very much. It makes one feel very grand indeed to have a man run ahead all the way to clear the people out of the road. It seems to be absolutely necessary in Tōkyō to have such a forerunner, for there are no sidewalks, and the streets are full of people, and especially of very small children, who are quite frequently burdened with smaller ones tied to their backs, so that they cannot get away with very great speed, and if the man did not run ahead to announce my coming, I could never go faster than a walk. On horseback the small size of everything in Japan is more than usually noticeable. Although the horse I rode to-day was a small one, I found that my view was rather more of the roofs than of the house fronts, and if I had ridden up close to a shop to make purchases, I think that my head would have come a good way above the eaves.

I have succeeded in securing as my Japanese teacher one of the officers of our school, who agrees to teach me Japanese in return for my teaching him English. He cannot speak a word of English, although he can read it quite easily. It seems that a good many Japanese learn English as we learn Latin and Greek, simply to read and for the sake of its literature, and never learn anything about its pronunciation, or to speak it or understand it when spoken.

October 11.

My afternoons have been chiefly occupied lately in getting a horse, as the first one I tried seemed rather small, and I was afraid he would break down under me. I have now in the stable a strong but not too beautiful black beast, who will, I hope, answer my purpose. His name is Dawn, though he is as black as night, and he has been a racer, and is said to run very well still, though the only time I have ridden him, so far, he did not condescend to show off his paces, but proceeded at the gravest and soberest of trots.

I have decided to take a class in the Sunday-school of one of the Japanese Congregational churches, if the pastor can get together one that would like to be taught in English. The pastor of this church, Mr. Kozaki, is an interesting man, and a very good specimen of the work turned out by the Doshisha School in Kyōtō. He is, I believe, the most influential Japanese Christian in Tōkyō, and has a large church which he has himself built up, and by which he is reaching more and more of the influential and educated Japanese. He speaks English easily and intelligibly, and seems to keep abreast of the most advanced religious thought.

There has never been a Congregational missionary stationed in Tōkyō, but two churches of that order have grown up here of their own accord, and are to-day more flourishing than many of those that have been built up and superintended by foreign missionaries resident in the city.

My Japanese is progressing, though not with great rapidity. The alphabet is quite discouraging. I find that the more letters I study, the fewer I can remember; and a curious psychological fact in regard to this study is that I can always remember the one next in order to the one I want. Then when I have at last found the one I am looking for and try to take the next one in order, I find that it has stepped out of its place in my head, leaving the next one to answer for it. It is very bewildering, and the only way I can catch the things is to make believe that I want the next-door neighbor, and then the one I am really looking for will sometimes come to me.

I started out on my ride this afternoon, taking Bruce for the first time. I had the groom warned beforehand that he was not to let the dog drink out of the ditches or bite the horse's legs. As a result of this warning, the poor man was nearly distracted with his complicated duties, for in his effort to run ahead and clear the way for me, and to keep track of Bruce and whip all the dogs that came running out to bark at him, he nearly exhausted himself. He was, however, very earnest and good natured in the performance of his work, and was much disgusted when Bruce succeeded in getting into a particularly nasty ditch before he could prevent it.

My groom is quite a picturesque looking fellow, with silky, slightly wavy hair, which he wears rather long and shakes back as he runs hatless through the streets, as if he were a little proud of it. He has a light, trim figure, which shows to advantage in his long blue tights and wing-sleeved blouse, belted around his slim waist with a dark blue sash. On a warm day, when he runs, he turns up his loose sleeves, showing a pair of well-shaped arms handsomely tattooed in blue and red. The first time he went out with me, I thought he had on a figured calico shirt, but a closer inspection showed that the figures were actually tattooed into his skin. To-day, when we reached home after our ride, I made the bettō wash Bruce, or rather I held the dog in the tub while the groom did the scrubbing. Poor Bruce had never taken a bath before such an audience in his life, and seemed grieved that I should make a fool of him in so public a way. The cook brought a large tub and placed it on the ground directly in front of my front door, and had filled it with water before I came out, so that I could not have it moved. Miné's whole family took up their station in my dining-room window, and the cook and his wife felt bound to stand around and see what was being done, while the groom and I attended to Bruce's toilet. I am sure that if any of my American friends could have come to see me just then, they would have thought the situation very funny.

Later in the afternoon, Miné and I went to a lecture on the volcanic explosion at Bandai San, given before the Seismological Society by one of the university professors. Though the professor was Japanese, the lecture was delivered in English, and illustrated with magic-lantern slides from photographs taken on the spot immediately after the eruption. Professor Sekiya estimated the area covered with mud as about twenty-seven square miles, and that covered with ashes as sixty-seven. He showed by a diagram how the whole top of the mountain was blown off and scattered in a shower of scalding mud over the surrounding country. He estimated that a billion and a half cubic yards of mud were poured out in this way. The country was completely inundated by streams of mud, carrying along on their surface enormous boulders. The river was dammed for a distance of ten miles, and spread itself out into three large lakes at places where its onward movement had been stopped, so increasing the destructive work of the explosion far beyond the mud-covered area. Seven villages were entirely destroyed, and a great extent of fertile land rendered for the present quite useless. Many lives were lost, and much suffering brought upon the survivors, who lost everything that goes to make life endurable.

As I was coming back from my ride this afternoon, I heard a shouting behind me, and knew that the carriage of some great person was approaching, so I drew up at the side of the road to let it pass, and to see if I could recognize any one in it. Two grooms ran ahead, shouting with all their might, a gorgeously liveried coachman sat on the box, and a footman, similarly attired, stood behind. There were three officers in full uniform in the carriage and one small boy, dressed in the uniform of the Peers' School, and with a knapsack strapped on his back. He stood up in the carriage to look at Bruce and me as he went by, and though he looked very much like any other small Japanese boy, I had a suspicion, from the pomp and circumstance with which he rode, that he might be Prince Haru. When he had passed, my groom turned to me and said in the Yokohama Japanese which grooms affect with their foreign employers, " Mikado no kodomo " (" the Mikado's boy "). I expressed interest, and he proceeded to enlighten me further with, " Him Nippon no ichi ban good boy," which is, being interpreted, " He is Japan's number one good boy."

Monday, October 15.

Yesterday morning, I tried to go to the English church in Shiba with a new jinrikisha man, who did not know the way at all. He dragged me pretty much all over Tōkyō, and frequently stopped and inquired the way, when I at once became the centre of an admiring crowd. The directions that he received always resulted in sending him straight up some particularly steep hill. After he had laboriously ascended, searched carefully upon the top for a church and found none, he would straightway bolt down the hill at break-neck speed and seek information elsewhere. In consequence of our researches on the various hilltops, I was ten minutes late at church, and had to walk in among the respectable and stiff English congregation when they were well on in the service.

In the evening, I went with Miné to an informal little service in the chapel of the Ladies' Institute, not far from our house.

I had been going on to take tea with a friend who lives the other side of Tōkyō, and had told my servants that I should not be back to dinner, but when the service was over I found it too late to go on, so went home, wondering whether I should have to go supperless to bed. However, Miné said that she had ordered for her supper some chicken and onions fried together in a peculiar Japanese way, and flavored with sugar, shōyu, and saké, and offered to share it with me. I sent my cook out to the nearest eel-house to order eels and rice, a dish which the Japanese cook to perfection, and we succeeded in making a very good supper on Japanese fare, pieced out with bread and knives and forks. The chicken, by the way, though it may not sound appetizing, was very good.

CHAPTER III.

OCTOBER 21 TO NOVEMBER 4.

Mr. Kozaki's Church. — Introduction to Bible Class. — Reception Days. — A Hibachi. — Two Old Ladies. — My Paper Dining-Room. — Funeral Fashions. — An Official Funeral. — Simplicity of Japanese Living. — Posthumous Titles. — The Emperor's Birthday.

Sunday, October 21, 1888.

THIS morning, in spite of a drenching rain, I attended service at the Japanese Congregational church near here, as steps had been taken to organize a class for me, and the pastor wanted me to come and meet my pupils. Although I could not understand a word of the service, I enjoyed it more than many meetings where English is spoken, for I sat where I could watch the audience, and their intentness made up somewhat for my lack of understanding. It was an intelligent-looking congregation, made up largely of men, most of them young, though here and there a gray head could be seen among the black ones. The people seemed to be drawn from all classes in society, although in this church there is a larger proportion of the official classes than in any other church in the city. It was most interesting to watch the audience during the sermon. All listened intently, and with more the look of students in a college lecture-room than of a congregation listening to a sermon. There was none of that air of polite boredom that we see so much of in American churches. Almost all the grown persons, both men and women, had Bibles, in which they verified carefully all references, and many had pencils and paper, with which they took notes. They were evidently in search of instruction rather than fine oratory or æsthetic gratification of any kind. The church was large and light and airy, with no attempt at ornament except the beautifully arranged flowers near the pulpit. The benches were exceedingly hard and uncomfortable, like all seats of Japanese manufacture. When the service was over, the pastor asked my class to meet me in a little room opening out of the main audience-room. When I went in, under his care, I was surprised to find some ten or a dozen exceedingly bright-looking young men awaiting me. They smiled and bowed, and seemed pleased to meet me, and after a little conversation we decided to take up the study of the Gospel of John, so next Sunday we begin with the first chapter.

One of my little peeresses has just sent me in a bunch of four magnificent chrysanthemums, the largest of them nearly the size of a peony. The chrysanthemums are just coming on now, but will be finer about the 1st of November. On November 3d, the Emperor's birthday, our school always goes over to the Emperor's garden to look at the chrysanthemums, which are then in their prime.

Monday, October 22.

To-day is our afternoon at home; for Miné and I have decided to have a day at home, for the sake of encouraging our friends to call on us. The distances are so great in Tōkyō that it is rather discouraging to any one to take a ride of an hour or two in jinrikisha to see a friend, and then find that friend out, so it has come to be the custom among the foreigners here to spend one afternoon in the week at home, and to serve a cup of tea to each guest.

On Saturday, Miné and I went to a kwan ko ba and bought a fine hibachi, or charcoal brazier, and a pretty copper tea-kettle, with a spray of cherry blossoms beaten out on it, in repoussé work, and Chinese letters in brass raised on the surface. Our hibachi is made of a section of a tree trunk, smoothed into a regular oval and hollowed out in the middle. The wood is about the color of old oak, and has a beautiful grain. Into the hollowed centre is set a copper pan. This is filled with light straw ashes, a little earthenware inverted tripod is pressed down into the ashes so that only the three points stick up, and then in the centre, between the three points, a charcoal fire is made. This smoulders away quietly under the tea-kettle placed on the tripod, and gives out neither smoke nor gas. The arrangement is very far superior to an alcohol lamp, as well as much cheaper, and why we do not use it in America I cannot imagine, except that we are not bright enough to think of such a simple thing; and, besides, we like the more complicated and expensive ways better. The curious thing about all these Japanese contrivances is that they are so simple that it seems as if any one might have thought of them, and yet they answer the purpose much better than many of our modern conveniences and inventions.

Miné has two old aunts spending the afternoon with her, and they have just been in to see me. They are both widows, and therefore wear their hair short. Neither of them had ever before been in a house furnished in foreign style, and they were much interested in walking about the room and examining everything minutely. At length we prevailed upon them to take chairs, upon the edges of which they sat gingerly, still craning their necks around in search of new wonders. I brought them tea, served not in Japanese but in foreign style, with saucers and spoons, and sugar and milk, and they heroically drank it, though I do not doubt they thought it nasty stuff. The cracker, which each took for the sake of politeness, was quite beyond them, so these were handed to Miné for Bruce, who sat up and went through his tricks in their honor, to their great entertainment. Then they toddled out, with many deep bows and arigato, apparently much gratified by their visit. I suppose it was as much of an event to them as it would be to us in America if we could suddenly step into a Japanese home, with everything in pure Japanese style.

We have had a change in the weather, and it has been quite cold to-day, as well as very damp, after our long storm. I have a fire in my parlor for the first time, and find that my eccentric little foreign stove (I think it must be German or French) works very well. My little paper dining-room is quite uncomfortably cold, and has no heating arrangement except hibachi. Two sides of the rooms are made entirely of sliding paper screens opening out of doors, so that it is very much exposed to the weather. There are wooden outside screens that can be closed, but they shut out the light, so I can only keep them closed when I wish to take my meals by lamplight. I have ordered new screens with glass set in them, and then I can let in the light and keep out the air, and hope to be able to make my dining-room comfortable, with a hibachi, in all but the worst weather.

October 25.

One of the high officials has just died, after a long illness, and he is to have a magnificent funeral, costing more than two thousand yen. He is to be buried at eight o'clock to-morrow morning, and as I do not have to be at school until 9.30, I shall try to get a look at the procession, which will be well worth seeing. It seems that when any one dies in Japan, all his friends send to his house gifts of money, fish, vegetables, fruit, cake, or eggs, as offerings to the spirit of the deceased, and if a man is in a prominent position and has many friends and retainers, the house is fairly flooded with these presents. Then, either thirty or fifty days after the death, the family give some kind of a feast in honor of the dead, and at that time they make great quantities of a certain kind of cake, which they send out to all the friends who have sent offerings. A funeral thus becomes a terrible expense both to the family and to all the friends and acquaintances of the deceased. Some of my Japanese friends with whom I was talking yesterday were inveighing against the custom as an utterly foolish one, particularly in a case like the present, for the high official whose death gave rise to this discussion of funeral customs leaves a large family, none too well off, and they are likely to be still further impoverished by the necessity of returning in some way the kindness of the friends who are at present sending in these extremely perishable offerings to the spirit of the departed. Inasmuch as probably not one in a hundred of the givers has the slightest belief that his gifts will be a benefit to the dead viscount's soul, but as they are all giving these things because their forefathers believed them necessary, it does seem absurd, not to say wicked, to keep up so useless and expensive a custom. As one of my friends said during the discussion, "Better bury him in a barrel,[1] than have his family impoverished by these ridiculous funeral customs." However, as it is likely to be a good deal of a show, and as my presence will not do much to encourage the nuisance, I think I shall take an early ride to-morrow and see what I can see.

[1] Among the poorest class of Japanese, the body, after death, is folded into a sitting posture, with the head bent forward, and placed in a wooden tub or cask for burial.

October 26.

I have been to the funeral, and though I did not have time to see the whole procession, still, what I saw was worth seeing. As Miné could not go with me, she sent two of her girls, and though they spoke very little English and could explain nothing, they were very polite and nice about showing me around and finding a good place for me to stay. It has been pouring all day, but, in spite of the rain, when we went out at eight o'clock this morning, the streets along the line of march were lined on both sides with people waiting patiently for a sight of the procession. We went in kurumas to a funny little house, in which lives the gate-keeper of the compound, or yashiki, where Miné used to live. The house, so far as I could see, and I think I saw the whole of it, consisted of three rooms: a living-room, that commanded a fine view of the street; a store-room, in which chests of clothes were stored, and where the bedding is kept during the day; and a kitchen, into which we could look, and in which we could see the family dining-trays piled up and the little fireplace set down into the floor. In the living-room there was a god-shelf, containing the family idols, with flowers set before them, and a little china cupboard, in which were the cheap but prettily decorated pieces of china that form the table service of any ordinary workingman's family. These things, with the omnipresent hibachi and tea-kettle, formed all the furniture of the room, except a pretty bamboo vase of autumn flowers that decorated the wall. Certainly, the independence of furniture displayed by the Japanese is most enviable, and frees their lives of many cares. Babies never fall out of bed, because there are no beds; they never tip themselves over in chairs, for a similar reason. There is nothing in the house to dust, nothing to move when you sweep; there is no dirt brought into the house on muddy boots; and it makes no difference whether the meals are served hot or cold, so long as there is hot water enough to make tea. The chief worries of a housekeeper's life are absolutely non-existent in Japan, except as they have been imported from abroad lately.

But this is a digression, and I must get back to the funeral. When we entered the house, we were greeted most cordially by a square, cheerful-looking little old woman, who went down on all fours and put her forehead to the ground as a token of her respect for us. We were given a very comfortable window, from which we could see far down the street, and catch the first glimpse of anything there was to be seen; so we sat there and waited, and watched the funny crowd that was gathered together under the windows. As soon as it became noised abroad that there was a foreigner in the house, the crowd became as much interested in the foreigner as they were in the expected funeral. The street soon began to present a lively appearance, as it filled up with the carriages of officials driving out to the cemetery, and with various lesser persons in kurumas, and military men on horseback. After a while groups of men, clothed in dark blue cotton blouses with curious white figures on them and gorgeous scarlet stripes on their shoulders, came sauntering by, some in kurumas, some on foot. They had some connection with the funeral, but what, I have not been able to discover. Then there was another wait, and at last there appeared twelve conical floral structures, each as large as a good-sized Christmas-tree, and each carried by two men. These passed, and were followed by more of the blue and red gentlemen before described. By this time I began to be uneasy lest I should be late to school, so at last, when the hands of my watch pointed to 9.30 and no sign of a procession was visible down the street, we were obliged to leave, much disappointed to have missed one of the greatest funeral processions ever seen in Tōkyō. But our disappointment was not destined to last very long, for just as we were turning off from the line of march the procession reached us, and we stopped to see it go by. First came the police force. It could hardly have been simply the Tōkyō force, for there were thousands of men. They looked very sombre, marching along in heavy ulsters, with pointed hoods drawn up over their heads to keep off the rain, — more like a company of cowled monks than policemen. After they had passed, there came a squad of soldiers, with white, bristly plumes in their caps, and one or two buglers, who played weird music of an extremely melancholy character. The instruments were European, but I think the music must have been Japanese. After the soldiers came a body of white-robed men, dressed like Shinto priests, and in their midst, carried by two bearers, a white, wooden box decorated with white paper, cut as one sees it in the Shinto temples. This box, which was quite large and carried like a kago, hung from a pole, supported on the shoulders of the bearers, I supposed at the time to be the coffin, but I learned afterwards that it contained valuables belonging to the deceased, which were to be buried with him. Behind the box came men carrying red and white flags, inscribed with the names and titles of the dead man, including his posthumous titles, given him by the Emperor immediately after death. I have seen by the papers that from the beginning of the illness of the dead viscount, the Emperor had been heaping titles and promotions upon him. The more hopeless his case became, the more honors he received, until, after his death, the highest title of all was bestowed.

Then followed an apparently endless procession of huge bouquets, like the first that had appeared an hour or more before the rest of the procession. These bouquets are sent as gifts by the friends of the deceased, and upon the standard of each is inscribed the name of the sender in large letters, that he who runs may read. In Japan, whoever sends flowers to a funeral hires also two white-robed men to carry his offering in the procession. It is this custom that forms a part of the great expense of Japanese funerals as now conducted, for the more flowers there are to carry through the streets, the greater the honor shown the dead.

That was all that I saw of the funeral, for when I was obliged to hurry off at last to my class, the street as far as I could see in either direction was a tossing tide of flowers, a beautiful sight in spite of the gray sky and heavy rain.

November 4.

Yesterday was the Emperor's birthday, one of the greatest holidays in the Japanese calendar. At half past seven o'clock Miné and I started out in our kurumas to go first to Yuki's house and pick up the children, and then out to the great parade ground at Aoyama to see the Emperor review the troops, on one of the few occasions when he appears in public as the actual commander of his own army. Even at that early hour the streets were very gay. The red and white Japanese flag adorned every house; the people were all out in their holiday clothes. Horsemen in dress uniforms, squads of soldiers furbished up in every possible way, courtiers and nobles in gold-laced court suits and cocked hats trimmed with gold lace and ostrich feathers, were hurrying in the direction of the parade ground. In the midst of the crowd we met our three little friends in their kurumas. They had started out early to come for us and save us the trouble of calling for them, so we turned around and went on with the stream of people, a crowd that grew larger and more picturesque as we came nearer to our destination. Thanks to the influence of friends at court, we were not halted on the edge of the ground like the rest of the crowd, but on presenting a pass were conducted by various deferential red-pantalooned soldiers along two sides of the great parade ground, and finally handed over to the Minister of War himself.

He was gorgeously dressed in a magnificent modern uniform heavily trimmed with gold lace, which made a great show on his ample chest, for he is a large man, unlike the majority of his countrymen. Wherever the gold lace did not cover his coat, he was adorned with orders and medals. He was delightfully polite to us, shook hands with me warmly, and conducted us into a tent next door to the Emperor's pavilion, where chairs were set, and where we waited a little while almost alone, for we were quite early, and hardly any one else had come. At last the tent began to fill up, and we found ourselves surrounded by princes, counts, viscounts, barons, foreign ministers, etc. I have not lived long enough in Japan to be much overpowered by titles, so I bore up bravely, and congratulated myself upon having so good a place from which to see what was going on. The glare of gold lace was something astonishing, and seemed to please the children very much. Perhaps the most interesting person to me in the company was a Chinese lady, the only real small-footed specimen that I have ever seen. She drove up to the tent in her carriage, from which she toddled with some difficulty to a seat, assisted on each side by a servant.

She had a doll-like face, delicately painted and shaped like the full moon, and was beautifully dressed in rustling silks, though the style of dress is to my mind not nearly so graceful as that of Japan. She sat only a little while in the tent, and long before the Emperor appeared or the show began, she toddled back to her carriage and drove away. Among the guests in the tent there were a few portly and impressive Chinamen in magnificent silk robes, members of the Chinese Legation, who strutted about with an air of owning the earth. It is that air that makes the Chinamen thoroughly hated by all outside nations with whom they have to do. Bōt' chan expressed the feeling they engender when he lifted his small finger wrathfully at one of the big Celestials, and said quite loudly in Japanese, "There's a Nankin foreigner. Kick him out!"

There were a good many English people there and a few Americans, so that much of the conversation was carried on in English, and it was quite a pleasure to be able to understand what people were saying. However, the foreigners were so tall that I had not the advantage of being able to see over their heads that I have in a Japanese crowd, and which I am beginning to regard as my natural right.

At last there was a sound of horses' hoofs and a blare of trumpets, and then every one began to try to push ahead of every one else, but, fortunately, we with the children were well in front, where we could see everything. A gorgeous state coach drove up, with two red-liveried men in front and two behind, and a mounted guard, with small red and white banners, galloping on each side. The coach stopped almost in front of us, and out of it came the Emperor himself, the direct descendant of the gods and the Son of Heaven, regarded still by his people as an object of worship. He did not look to me so very different from other people. He is lighter than the average Japanese man, or rather, I should say he looked to me lighter, because I have heard other foreigners say that he is really darker than most of his people. His features are strongly marked and heavy — something after the Inca type; perhaps because both the Mikados and the Inca kings claim to be "Children of the Sun."

When the Emperor had gone into his pavilion, the coach drove away, and the generals and staff officers came hurrying by to mount their horses. Bōt' chan spied his father among the others and made a wild rush after him, but was caught and brought back to his place by his valet, while the whole company of hurrying officers shouted over his escapade. Soon there was another blare of trumpets, and a gorgeous company rode by on horseback. First came the standard-bearer with the imperial ensign, a white chrysanthemum on a red silk ground. Then on a graceful little brown Arab with gold bridle and trappings rode his Imperial Majesty. He is a skillful and daring horseman, it is said, but he rides in the old Japanese style, sitting all in a heap like a bag of meal, his legs dangling straight down on each side of the horse, and his elbows twitching and jerking with every motion of the animal. Even a descendant of the gods and Son of Heaven could not make this style of riding dignified, according to our ideas. After the Emperor came the generals, with the Minister of War at the head, and the whole party made the circuit of the field together, coming back to take up their station close by us, so near that if I had had anything to say to the Emperor I could have said it without raising my voice. There he sat for an hour or more, while the troops marched by him; and as a very large proportion of the entire Japanese army is stationed in Tōkyō, this really gave me time to study the Emperor's appearance and dress pretty carefully. He wore a very fine uniform, not unlike that of his officers, except that he had a wider gold belt than the rest and a fluffier plume on his cap. He could be distinguished anywhere in the field from the others by a broad pink band, which passed from his waist over his right shoulder, and by the more gorgeous trappings of his horse. It seems that on his birthday the Emperor has an exhausting time of it. He has to get up at two o'clock in the morning, bathe himself in a careful and ceremonial manner, and dress himself in some peculiar and ancient costume. Thus attired, and accompanied by the high officers of his household, he repairs to a shrine within the court inclosure, and there performs a solemn service to the souls of his ancestors. This must be done fasting.

The Emperor enters the shrine alone, his officers waiting without during the ceremony.

This done, Old Japan steps aside for a while, and the Emperor of New Japan must change his antique dress and don the modern uniform, and show himself before all the people, as he sits for hours on his little Arab, reviewing his thousands of well-disciplined troops with their modern arms, uniforms, and accoutrements. When that is over, he goes back to the palace, takes breakfast with his ministers, and receives all his officers, high and low. This programme keeps him busy from early in the morning until some time in the afternoon, and makes as long and tiresome a day's work as any emperor would care to perform, I should think.

The review was over at last, and a most uncommonly good show it was; the Emperor dismounted and stepped into his carriage, and the red and white banners, the black horses, the red coachmen, and the gorgeous coach vanished amid the blowing of trumpets and the lifting of hats. Then there was a scramble to see who would get off the field first. We sent for our kurumas to come to us, as we did not like to take the little children through the crowd, but after waiting for nearly half an hour Miné hired another kuruma and hurried off to school, while I, with the two little ones and two men-servants, plunged into the crowd, where we at last found our kurumas and went home. There was only time to change my dress, eat my lunch, and hurry over to school for the afternoon exercises. The pupils were all there, and the guests had begun to arrive, when I reached the schoolhouse, and all looked very gay and festive in their best dresses, though some of the efforts at foreign dress were rather pathetic than beautiful. The whole school was obliged to spend an unconscionable time waiting in the playground for the signal to be given us to go into the assembly room. It was cold, and we had neither wraps nor head coverings, and it seemed to me a cruel exposure of so many delicate girls. At last, however, we were allowed to march into the open and chilly gymnasium that serves the school for an assembly room. All the pupils sat together, and the teachers together, and then facing them, in the place where the platform would have been if there had been any, were chairs for the visitors. These soon began to be filled with gorgeous beings in court suits, fathers of our girls, who had come over to see us after paying their respects to the Emperor. There were also a few ladies, mothers of our children, handsomely dressed in foreign costumes, many of them probably imported from Paris. When all were seated, a chord on the piano gave the signal for the teachers and pupils to rise; at a second chord we bowed to our guests, and at a third we sat down.

The first performance on the programme was a song, the words of which were composed by Baron Takasaki, the court poet, and the music by one of the court musicians. It was written expressly for the day, and sung by all the schools throughout the country. The music, though composed by a Japanese, is in foreign style, and the words are rhythmically arranged, though I do not think they are made to rhyme.

When Japanese attempt to sing foreign music, they do not exactly sing, they buzz. There is a peculiar quality in their voices that reminds me of the description of the song of the Bluebottle Flies in Edward Lear's delightful "Nonsense Book." Our scholars sang this song with great mechanical precision, but absolutely without expression or any apparent enjoyment. It was as different as possible from the singing of our Hampton pickaninnies, with their sweet, clear voices and pathetic quickness of sympathy with the feeling of the music.

During the singing the gold-laced audience looked a little bored, and were distinctly relieved when it was over. Then three little girls came forward and seated themselves at three kotos, that were arranged in front of the audience.

The koto is the Japanese piano, a long, stringed instrument, lying horizontally, and played with ivory tips fastened to the fingers. It is to me much the most agreeable of Japanese instruments, and has considerable power to soothe even my savage breast. It is very pretty to watch three performers playing together as these children did, for the motions are exceedingly graceful, rather more like those of a harper than a pianist. The little girls sang a

Japanese song, very high and nasal, but with some pleasing strains.

Other musical performances followed, the Japanese and foreign styles alternating on the programme, and at last the school, teachers, and guests rose, and all heads were bowed while the school sang the little song written expressly for them by the Empress herself. Then the guests departed and the girls marched out, and everything was over. It took some time for all our magnificent visitors to get into their carriages and off, and after they were gone the Japanese teachers stayed and ate some lunch that had been sent over from the palace to the school, what was left from the Emperor's breakfast. I did not stay, as I had had my lunch before coming to school, and the teachers warned me that the imperial lunch was not likely to suit the foreign palate. I took with me when I went home a marvelous box of candy, containing two perfectly imitated green oranges, each with a little bunch of leaves, a large white sugar chrysanthemum, and a lump of green bean marmalade, frosted with pink, sweet vermicelli. I presented them this morning to my cook to give his children, as, though they were beautiful to look at, they were too sweet and tasteless to suit the foreign palate.

CHAPTER IV.

November 12 to 14.

A Nō Performance. — Death of Prince Aki. — Dango Zaka.

Tōkyō, November 12, 1888.

LAST Wednesday I went to a Nō performance, and enjoyed it immensely. The Nō is a musical and theatrical performance, somewhat religious in its character, I believe, and very ancient in its origin. It is the only theatrical performance that it is proper for the Empress and the higher nobility to attend. The Nō is held very often in this city on Sunday, but so far I had not attended it, as I still prefer to take entertainments of a dramatic kind on week-days, and to keep my Sundays for other uses. Fortunately, however, for me and my principles, Yuki discovered that there was to be a special performance on the occasion of the annual festival at a shrine not far from where we live; so, though she could not go herself, she sent one of her servants with me to take care of me, and I had a very pleasant afternoon.

The approach to the place was about as entertaining as the show itself, for all the streets surrounding the temple inclosure were crowded with people, and on each side of the street were little booths, some containing toys and other knickknacks for sale, and others the headquarters of small side-shows. The nature and attractions of these shows were set forth in pictures hung without the booths, after the manner of the " pink-eyed lady, Proosian dwarf, and livin' skeleton " of our own circuses, except that the pictures were of such a new and interesting character that I should certainly have spent most of the afternoon in looking at the side-shows, if my guide had understood English, and I could have made him know what I wanted. As it was, I could not stop, but went on through the funny crowd, and by the funny pictures, into the great inclosure where the main show was to be held. Here we alighted from our kurumas and walked, followed by the usual multitude, for my personal appearance excites great interest among the plebeian Japanese. There was an immense concourse in one part of the temple grounds, and toward this nucleus all new-comers seemed to be drifting. To the edge of this we also drifted, and here the man left me for a few minutes, while he went off to secure me a seat. When he came back, I was the centre of a group of children, who had gathered about me and were carefully studying every detail of my costume. He drove the children away, and carried me off and over to the temple itself. Up and down the long, steep flights of steps were streams of people ascending and descending, like the angels on Jacob's ladder. Here my escort left me again, and at once all the angels deserted the ladder and came crowding about me, while I stood and tried to look as if I were unconscious of everything for about ten minutes. At the end of that time my guide returned, and brought with him a man carrying a ticket and a chair. Then we moved on, but in a moment or two stopped at a small house, from which the man with the ticket procured a coolie to carry the chair. Once more we moved on, the chair-coolie in front, the ticket man next,

I meekly following him, and my original escort guarding the rear of the procession. Soon we were in the thick of the crowd and squirming our way through it, the coolie in advance, grunting fiercely, and using the chair as an entering wedge. We found ourselves after a while under a kind of scaffolding loaded with people. The coolie climbed up a short ladder and through a very small hole, deposited the chair, and came back. Then the ticket-man indicated to me that I was to climb the ladder, which I did. But when it came to crawling through the small hole, with my high hat and my bulky foreign dress, I could not do it. First I stove in the crown of my hat, then I stuck igno-miniously, with my head and shoulders through the hole, until a kindly soldier above and my own retainers below succeeded in pulling and pushing me through. Once through, I found myself in the best seat in the place. You cannot call it a house, because, though the scaffolding on which I sat was roofed over, most of the audience sat on the ground out of doors. This scaffolding, through the floor of which I had been so laboriously pushed and pulled, was built in the form of a hollow square, three sides of which, roofed over and divided into boxes, formed the grand stand for the *élite* of the audience. The fourth side contained the stage, a roofed and matted square, joined with the dressing-room at the left by an open gallery, in which much of the action of the play took place. The dressing-room was separated from this gallery by a curtain, which was lifted for the performers to make their entrances and exits, but kept closed the rest of the time. The actor often began to sing or speak while still in the dressing-room, and in making his entrance could be seen walking very slowly along the gallery on his way to the stage, which occupied the centre of its side of the square. A little door at the right of the stage occasionally afforded means of exit for the actors. The space between this door and the corner was screened from the public gaze by a high board fence. The whole space between the private boxes on the scaffolding and the stage was unroofed and unfloored, but filled with the common people, seated on mats on the ground, eating, drinking tea, smoking, and walking about in the most delightfully sociable manner. It was fun enough to watch this part of the audience when there was nothing especially interesting being done on the stage.

At my left, a box draped with purple curtains, upon which was stamped the white chrysanthemum, was evidently reserved for the imperial family. Prince Haru occupied it for a little while, but during most of the afternoon it was vacant.

Though I had no one to explain anything to me, I found the performance most interesting. It was something like the ancient Greek drama in many ways, but in other respects perhaps more like the early English plays. During most of the performances there was a chorus of some twenty uniformed men, dressed in dark blue with some lighter blue decorations. These men sat motionless on the floor at the right of the stage, in two lines, and never stirred from the beginning to the end of the scene. They sang occasionally, very sweetly, sometimes alone, sometimes as a sort of accompaniment to some of the actors. There were three or four instrumental musicians, too, who sat on stools at the back of the stage. Their instruments were mostly drums, shaped like hour-glasses, but there was one man who played a pipe. The drummers held their drums on their knees and spanked them with the palms of their hands, and at the same time gave vent to yells or howls that sounded as cheerful and musical as the wail of a homesick dog.

At the left, at the very back of the stage, as close against the wall as they could sit, were two or three men dressed exactly like the musicians, whose *raison d'être* I did not at first discover. I found out, however, as the performance went on, that these men were dressers to the actors, who went and stood in front of them, and with their backs to the audience, when they were in need of repairs or slight changes of costume of any kind. Beside this, the men occasionally moved stealthily across the stage to pick up and remove anything dropped by the actors that would not be needed again, thus keeping the stage tidy all the time.

So much for the stage and its furnishings: now for the performances. When I reached the place, the programme was already under way, and a weird figure in a mask, with a profusion of long, black hair, was holding a musical controversy with two elderly gentlemen, assisted by the chorus and the drummers. I could not understand much about it, but the dispute seemed to end in the complete rout of the long-haired demon, who fled ingloriously off the stage, followed by his two opponents and the chorus and orchestra.

The next scene was a sort of a farce, as nearly as I could judge, and in this scene there was no chorus. There was a fine young lord with two retainers, to whom he seemed to be giving orders. One of these retainers was the funny man, and he certainly was very funny. After a good many speeches, by which he put the audience into roars of laughter, and during which his tones, looks, and gestures were enough to keep me thoroughly amused, he went to the back of the stage, took a piece of white cloth from one of the motionless propertymen, and brought it forward to his master. Then they both sat down, and he went vigorously to work twisting the piece of white cloth into a rope. But he was so very fond of hearing his own voice that he kept forgetting his work, and then coming back to it with a great show of industry. After a while the master got up and stole quietly out, but the servant kept on addressing the audience in the most confidential manner, twisting away on his work spasmodically. While he was talking, the other servant came quietly in and sat down behind the talker, who was entirely unconscious of his presence. The listener at last became much excited over some revelations that the old gabbler was making, and listened eagerly, then lifted his hand to strike the man, but refrained through his desire to hear more. The old fellow talked on, utterly unconscious of the pantomime that was being enacted behind his back, until at last his fellow-servant could restrain his rage no longer and struck the old rogue. Then there was a lively scene. The talker was a coward. He begged pardon. He ran around the stage. He did everything he could to show that he was sorry. But his fellow-servant was obdurate, and chased him off the stage amid the delighted roars of the audience. The old man's acting was wonderfully good, as, indeed, was all the acting that I saw.

The next scene was, I think, historical, taking up some events in the early life of Yoshitsuné, one of Japan's greatest heroes.

The principal performer was a little boy, who took the part of Yoshitsuné. He had a sweet, high voice, which varied pleasantly the monotony of the men's deep chanting. In this scene the chorus and orchestra were once more in their places. The first part of the act was stately and solemn, but toward the end Yoshitsuné took up his stand at the right of the stage, in the corner, just in front of the orchestra, and there with drawn sword awaited whoever might try to pass. It was supposed to be dark, although the sun was actually shining directly on the stage. After Yoshitsuné had stood in the corner a little while, three strange figures issued from the dressing-room and crept slowly along the gallery. They were dressed in the most fantastic manner, and I am not sure whether they were intended for beggars or highwaymen. When they came to the end of the gallery, they halted, peered forward into the imaginary darkness of the stage, and at last seemed to conclude that they needed lights. So they turned their backs to the audience, and the convenient property-men supplied each of them with a stick, at the end of which a tassel of red horsehair represented the flame of a torch. After some hesitation and talk, one of the men groped his way on to the stage, waving his horsehair torch wildly before him. He gradually felt his way across to the spot where Yoshitsuné was standing, and thrust his horsehair torch into the very face of the little hero, who thereupon lifted his sword and knocked the torch out of the man's hand. The man himself, scared out of his wits, rolled over and over on the floor, and at last crawled, yelling, back to his companions, and told them of his terrifying adventure. The others laughed at him and made great game of him, and a second one essayed to brave the terrors of the stage. He came on a little more boldly than his predecessor, but still with great circumspection. When he came near Yoshitsuné's corner, the boy lifted his foot and brought it down with a sudden stamp, and the poor beggar was so alarmed that he dropped his torch, rolled over on his back, and there lay howling helplessly, until his companions came and dragged him back to the gallery again. Then the third man came on, and received such a thrashing from the little boy that he was carried off by his friends almost insensible. Discouraged by this last repulse, the three beggars went out of the little door at the right, leaving Yoshitsuné once more in solitary possession of the stage. But very soon the dressing-room curtain was raised, and an imposing procession of warriors, armed with swords and spears, came marching slowly along the gallery. They were dressed in armor, and were led by a ferocious-looking captain. They stopped in the gallery just before reaching the stage and held a council of war, as a result of which a big fellow with a long spear was sent ahead to reconnoitre. He groped his way cautiously forward through the darkness, but was met in the middle of the stage by the small boy, who fell upon him with his short sword, avoiding the thrusts of the warrior's long spear by nimbly hopping over it, as if it were a skipping rope. It was a most comical fencing match, varied by the big warrior's turning somersaults over his own spear, like a clown at a circus. He was finally killed, and another warrior came forward to take his place, when the dead man picked himself up and ran off the stage, making his exit by the little door on the right. Then the little boy fought single-handed all the warriors in the gallery, sometimes vanquishing two at a time. All the fencing matches were varied by most extraordinary tumbling, which excited the greatest enthusiasm on the part of the audience. When the small boy had chased his last enemy, the fierce-looking leader of the band, along the gallery and into the dressing-room, the fight was ended.

The next scene was to me the funniest of all, perhaps because I could understand it better than the rest. It was after this manner. A samurai gentleman appears on the scene and soliloquizes for a little while. Then the dressing-room curtain opens and a most attractive figure comes gliding along the gallery. It is slender and graceful, and elegantly arrayed in a brocaded silk kimono, but its head is covered by a beautiful white satin gown, which falls over the face, and is evidently held in place by the wearer's hands. Suddenly the samurai catches sight of the gliding figure, and is evidently smitten by it. He apostrophizes it and tries to induce it to come nearer, but it refuses, and at last glides silently back to the dressing-room.

The samurai gentleman is much disappointed, and confides his grief to the audience in a long speech. As suddenly as before, the figure appears again, this time at the right-hand door, glides forward to the centre of the stage, and stands close to the man before he becomes aware of its presence. When he sees that the mysterious being has returned, he utters a squeal of joyful surprise, and addresses it. He is evidently trying to make her show her face, but she shakes her head and refuses. Then he takes her by the shoulders and walks her around the stage, talking to her coaxingly the while, but she is still obdurate. At last they both sit down, he continuing his efforts to make her show her face, but without success. After a while he loses patience, rushes at her, and tears the wrapping from her head, then drops it and flees precipitately across the stage, for the face is a hideous, distorted, and discolored mask. He has evidently been wasting his attentions on a demon of the most unpleasant type. The unveiled demon pursues him and grasps him by the arm; he pushes it away, but the demon, not in the least discouraged, attacks him again, and, overcome with terror, the valiant samurai runs off the stage, closely pursued by his uncanny visitor.

There was one more scene, but it was quite dark on the stage by the time the performance was over, so I did not get much idea of it, except that there was a great deal of fighting in it. I have written out a somewhat detailed description of the afternoon's performances, but with all I have said I am afraid I have given no idea of the gorgeous costumes, the curious music, and the graceful, measured movements of the actors, which gave to the entertainment the character of a dance as well as of a play.

We were to have gone to the Emperor's gardens to-day to see the chrysanthemums, but the death of the Emperor's youngest son, little Prince Aki, has put a stop to all festivities for the present.

November 14.

Although the little prince died on Saturday, for some inscrutable reason the official announcement of his death was not made until Monday night, and then it stated that he died at half past two on Monday, in spite of the fact that every one knows that he died on Saturday. When our school assembled on Tuesday morning, the announcement was made to the pupils, and they were dismissed immediately.

Yesterday afternoon I went down to Dango Zaka to see the chrysanthemum show, which is one of the sights of Tōkyō at this season. It is an extraordinary sight, and quite peculiar to Japan. Beside the beautiful display of potted chrysanthemums of wonderful colors and shapes, there are numerous scenes, historical, mythological, etc., in which the figures and landscapes are constructed entirely of chrysanthemums. The heads, feet, and hands of the human figures are of papier-maché, or some similar composition, and very lifelike, but the draperies, mountains, waterfalls, and animals are constructed entirely of these plants, their many-colored flowers woven into solid masses. Among the scenes represented there was a goddess rising from the waves and showing herself to an excited group of men in a balcony; the gods dancing before the cave into which the sun goddess had retired to sulk; Taiko Sama with the infant Mikado in his arms receiving the unwilling homage of the court; a Buddhist monk seated under an immense green and white waterfall and watched over by guardian spirits in mid-air; a white elephant with a gayly dressed lady on his back; and even Bandai San in a state of violent eruption. These are only a few of the many scenes scattered through various matted sheds, so many and so large that it was an afternoon's work to visit them all. I had the good fortune to find a man engaged in repairing one of the figures, or rather its garment, composed entirely of small, yellow flowers scattered about on a background of green leaves. I watched him long enough to see exactly how the thing was put together. There is a bamboo framework in the required shape, with papier-maché head, hands, and feet. Into this framework are put whole plants in full flower, their roots packed with damp earth and bound about with bits of soft straw matting. The stems, with the leaves and flowers, are then pulled through to the outside of the frame, and woven by dexterous fingers into the desired pattern. The figures are kept in the shade and watered as they need it, and the plant goes on growing and blossoming as happily as if it were not forming part of a drapery. These flower structures, as you see, are quite different in principle from those of our own floral designs, in which the flowers are snipped off, run through with wires, fastened to toothpicks, and stuck into their places, to wither and die prematurely, for the sake of a few hours' decoration.

CHAPTER V.

November 25 to December 18.

A Ball at the Rokumei-kwan. — A Tōkyō Story. — Bōt' chan's Studies in Physiognomy. — Thanksgiving and Turkey. — Christmas Carols. — Fuji-Yama. — The New Palace. — Tōkyō Moats. — Bowing to Prince Haru.

Tōkyō, November 25, 1888.

The past week has been quite a gay one in my quiet life. I do not know whether I told you that I had been invited to a ball given by one of the cabinet ministers. It was held at the Rokumei-kwan, or Nobles' Club. The building is in foreign style, and handsomely fitted up with foreign furniture. It was beautifully decorated for the occasion with plants, flowers, and flags, and the grounds were illuminated with lanterns. The ball was given for the foreign naval officers, and was not a very large one, — only four or five hundred invitations issued, — so the rooms were not at all crowded. At such an entertainment as this there is one drawing-room and a small dining-room set apart for the aristocracy, — princes, princesses, counts, countesses, etc. From this retreat the nobility come out and mingle with the crowd when they like, but the crowd is not expected to go in and mingle with the nobility to any great extent. I went to the ball under the escort of some American friends, and our first duty was to hunt up our host and hostess, who had already stopped receiving when we arrived at half past nine, and retired to the aristocratic penetralia before mentioned. Led by my more daring escort, I ventured in thither, and there saw the princesses all sitting in a row, looking very uncomfortable in their stiff, foreign dresses, and quite bored beside. The princes were mostly outside dancing with the multitude, and when we returned to the ball-room my friends pointed them out. They did not seem to me very impressive in appearance, but have an exceedingly aristocratic way of holding up their heads that makes up somewhat for their small stature.

The thing that struck me most on going into the dancing-room was the amazing number of men in gorgeous uniforms and the very small sprinkling of ladies, mainly foreign, and all in foreign dress. There was an open space in the centre of the floor, in which the dancers enjoyed themselves, and around the edges was a solid phalanx of men, looking on at the evolutions of their brethren who had been fortunate enough to secure partners. Apropos of the small number of women, I heard rather a funny story from a lively little Japanese lady to whom I was introduced. She spoke English prettily, though with a strong accent, and was being instructed in the latest style in foreign clothes by an American friend when I came up. When I remarked to her on the small number of ladies present, she laughed heartily as she told me of a gentleman who had come to her that evening and asked her to find him a young lady as a partner. She said that she did not know any young lady whose card was not already full. " Well, then," was the reply, " find me an old lady, for I must dance." But no old lady could be found, so the would-be dancer was obliged to join the ranks of the male wall-flowers who formed so noticeable a feature of the affair.

As I do not dance, I should not care to go to many balls, but once in a while it is fun to stand by and watch the world enjoy itself. We left at about one, and had a beautiful moonlight ride home through the quiet streets, in an air as warm and soft as that of a summer night among the New England hills.

I think I must be in high favor with the missionaries of Tōkyō, for this is the story that is afloat in missionary circles about me: Before I came to Japan I was engaged in training theological students for the ministry, and when I received my invitation to teach in the Peeresses' School, I at once wrote back that I would not come unless I was allowed to teach Christianity. My answer was laid before the Empress, who deliberated over it awhile, and at last said, "Let her come;" so I came. I shudder to think how I would fall in the estimation of those who believe this story, if they knew that the conditions I made were not in regard to teaching Christianity, but were in regard to dogs and horses. I do not know whether the story was imported from America, or whether it is a native of Japanese soil, but it just shows how little any story is to be trusted that is told in this part of the world. It is the merest matter of luck that the story is not to my discredit. If it were, it would be believed just as readily, and with just as little pains taken to prove or disprove it.

Yuki's little boy regards me with great favor, partly because I ride horseback, and partly because I am so different from the rest of his small world. Now, whenever I go to see his mother, he meets me at the door and escorts me upstairs. When I sit down, he draws a chair up close to mine, sits down in it, and takes my hand. This he holds sentimentally for a while, sitting with his eyes fixed on my face, scrutinizing carefully the points of difference between me and his other friends. Then he stands up in his chair and leans over to me with his mouth puckered up for a kiss. When I have kissed him, he grows bolder, and stretches out his chubby hand to pat and smooth my cheeks. I think that the color of my face was what led him to begin this patting, — he wanted to see if it rubbed off; but now, though he has satisfied himself on that point, he seems to enjoy feeling of me. Then he passes his little fingers all around my eye-sockets, with a view to ascertaining whether they really are as deep-set and hollow as they look. When his investigations are ended, he cuddles up close to me, and sits quite still for a long time, by way of showing his satisfaction; a great honor, for he is a very lively little boy, and rarely sits still for a minute. He calls me Bacon Chan, a kind of diminutive of Bacon San, or Miss Bacon.

December 2.

The weather is really growing quite wintry, and to-day I noticed that the banana-trees in our garden, which have kept green and bright until now, are withered by the frost, and look forlorn enough.

My Thanksgiving dinner last week was quite a success. My cook was not equal to the real American dishes required for the occasion, so I had to do a large part of the preparation myself, but was rewarded for my labors over chicken pie, boiled turkey with oyster sauce, celery salad, pumpkin pie, etc., by the evident gusto with which my Americo-Japanese friends partook of the feast, and by the remark of one of them that it tasted like home, meaning the old home in America in which much of her girlhood had been passed. Thanksgiving Day was a busy one for me. School in the morning, preparation of the dinner until nearly four, dinner at home at four, and a second dinner with foreign friends at seven.

I had rather a funny time about my turkey. I told my cook a week beforehand that I must have one for Thanksgiving Day, but as turkeys are very expensive out here, and Cook San is an economical soul, I think he hoped I would forget my contemplated extravagance. When I came home from school on Wednesday, I made inquiries about my *pièce de resistance*, and found that it had not yet been procured, so I sent Cook San out in haste to secure it. I was sitting in my parlor not long afterward, writing, when I heard a gentle "quit" in the hall, and there was my cook with a cheerful-looking turkey hen under his arm. The bird was evidently quite used to being handled, and was looking about with an air of mild surprise and interest in its new surroundings that was really pathetic. I requested the cook to have the poor thing killed at once, but shortly afterward, as I was at work moulding piecrust in the dining-room, I spied my turkey peacefully grazing in the door-yard. I once more sent for the cook, pointed severely at the turkey, and requested him to kill it. This time he took my advice, but I think he would have greatly preferred to allow the bird to enjoy life until an hour before dinner.

Miné and I, aided by the very eccentric and tuneless piano that came with the house, have undertaken to teach one or two Christmas hymns in English to some of the young people of the church, and hereafter they are to come every Sunday afternoon to practice. Neither Miné nor I are very skillful musicians, but Miné can play the tunes on the piano, and I can keep both time and tune with my voice, and both of these are quite rare accomplishments in this part of the world.

I do not think I have written you much of anything about Fuji-Yama, but now that the clear winter weather has set in, it has become a conspicuous object in the landscape. During the summer, the mountain is not often visible from Tōkyō, as the air is too hazy, but now, although eighty miles away, it looms up on the horizon from every high point in the city. In the morning one can see even the blue hollows in the snow that covers its sides, and at sunset it rises, a great purple cone, against the golden southwestern sky. I do not wonder that the Japanese love the mountain and picture it so often, for it is so majestic in its solitary height, so symmetrical in its outline, so continually changing in its aspect, that it becomes a part of one's life here, and after a little one comes to regard it as a personal presence, and not simply as an object in the landscape. Yesterday, when I went to Yokohama, the mountain was surrounded by clouds that filled in the gap between it and the nearer and lower Hakoné mountains. From this garment of cloud, the hoary, sunlit head towered far into the blue sky. To-night, as I was riding homeward through the crowded city streets, I turned a corner and there in front of me was the Hakoné range, blue and mysterious in the sunset light, and Fuji's whole perfect outline overlooking and dwarfing them all, and the new moon and the evening star shining above him in the crimson sky. Then in a moment the street crooked again, and he was gone.

December 18.

Last week Wednesday the school was invited to visit the new palace, which is now finished and furnished and ready for occupancy, — only waiting until the court can persuade His Majesty to move in, a step which, at present, he utterly declines to take. So, in the mean time, various fortunate sorts and conditions of men are invited to come and take a look at the grandeur that the Mikado will none of. Our school was invited at twelve o'clock, so as to see it all and get through before the boys should arrive at two. School closed at half past eleven, but there was some difficulty in loading two hundred and fifty children into two hundred and fifty kurumas, each in her own private conveyance, and all in the order of their rank in the school, and then in engineering this line of two hundred and fifty kurumas single file through the crowded streets to the palace. It was a funny sight when at last we were off, and our long, black line squirmed around the curves of the moats, looking like a procession of ants. I was near the end of the procession, so I could see it nicely, and I never before felt quite as much as if I were part of a circus. Our way lay through Kōjimachi, one of the great business streets, and all the tradespeople turned out of their shops and stood in the streets to see us go by. We left our kurumas outside of the outer gate of the main entrance to the palace grounds, crossed two magnificent bridges that span the wide moat, and then found ourselves within the palace inclosure.

The moats of Tōkyō are, to my mind, the most beautiful things in the city, with their almost perpendicular green banks dropping down to the fine, stone-faced channels in which the water lies. The banks are planted with magnificent pines, and at this season the glassy water is covered with wild fowl, swimming about as securely in the heart of this city of a million inhabitants as if they were in the wildest of mountain tarns. The moats are particularly beautiful where we crossed them, and their picturesqueness is increased by the high walls and antique Japanese towers of the old Shōgun's castle, for the new palace is built on the site of the old Tokugawa castle, and the Tokugawa fortifications still surround it, though the castle itself was burned in 1868.

We had to walk quite a distance, and over round pebbles, large enough to make walking on them most uncomfortable, before we reached the palace, and then it took some time to get our long line in, as there was a great polishing of shoes with handkerchiefs, lest a particle of dust from them should soil the sacred precincts. I saw the palace last summer very thoroughly, before it was finished and furnished, and admired then the exquisite carved, lacquered, painted, and embroidered work with which it is decorated; but I doubted then whether the small, shabby iron grates that have been put into some of the finest rooms, and the gorgeous foreign upholstery which then stood unpacked, ready to be put in place, would add greatly to the beauty of the Emperor's new abode. Now that everything is in order, it looks much better than I had expected it would. The throne room is really magnificent. The palace is built on a purely Japanese plan, with long verandas or corridors opening upon gardens or court-yards, although glass doors stand in the place of the old-fashioned paper shoji, and there is the modern improvement of a basement containing steam-heating apparatus, while the dim illumination of the andon is replaced by the glare of multitudinous electric lights set in chandeliers ablaze with crystal brilliants.

The girls were much impressed and interested, and we went so slowly that we saw, as we looked back across gardens to the corridors or verandas along which we had come, that the boys of the Peers' School were beginning to come in before we were half through. They traveled from room to room, and from corridor to corridor, in a business-like and perfunctory way that brought them constantly nearer to us. Pretty soon a messenger brought us word that Prince Haru was among the boys, and that if they caught up with us we must all stop and bow until he had passed by. We hurried, after that, and tried to finish and get out before the boys came along; but as girls take more interest in upholstery than boys, the peers gained on the peeresses, and we were just outside of the door and preparing to march, when there was a cry of "Miya Sama!" ("the Prince!") and down we all went, bending ourselves double, all for the sake of a very minute boy in a little school uniform, with a little school knapsack on his back, as much like the other boys he was with as if they had been manufactured by the dozen. I must say, that rather went against the grain with me. I don't mind bowing to officials and dignitaries, but when it comes to doubling myself up in an abject manner before a boy of seven, I don't like it. However, when one is with peeresses, one must do as the peeresses do, so I put my pride in my pocket, stood behind my pupils, and bowed with the rest.

CHAPTER VI.

DECEMBER 27 TO JANUARY 6.

Christmas Preparations. — Hanging Stockings. — English Service. — A Church Festival. — New Year's Decorations. — New Year's Eve on Ginza. — A Street Fight. — New Year's Day. — Street Performers. — An Earthquake. — Kurumayas in Cold Weather.

TŌKYŌ, December 27, 1888.

CHRISTMAS is safely over, and our vacation is a pleasant relief after the steady grind of school and the wear and tear of Christmas preparation. It may seem to you as if out here I might get away from the annual madness of Christmas giving, and it was quite a surprise to me to see what a number of presents I wished to make. My own household alone consists of twelve persons, for my cook has three children and my groom five, and these with the four heads of the two families make a round dozen. Then Miné's household adds five more under the same roof with me, with whom I am thrown into most intimate relations. Added to these are many outside friends who have shown me great kindness since I came here, so that Christmas seemed a good time to evince my appreciation of their favors.

Shopping is not by any means as easy here as at home, for I have either to go to Yokohama for things, or else to get them one at a time at the shops in Tōkyō, which are all very far apart, and all a half day's journey from my house. I went to Yokohama twice, and did the rest of my shopping in Tōkyō, accomplishing very little in an afternoon, both on account of the magnificent distances and the slowness of Japanese shopkeepers. However, by dint of great exertions, I did succeed in securing a number of pretty things by Christmas Eve, and Miné and I worked until quite late at night, tying up our presents in proper shape with the red and white paper strings, and the bit of dried fish done up in bright paper that must always go with a present in Japan.

Miné wished her household to have the pleasure of hanging up stockings, so for lack of a chimney we hung them on the chairs in my parlor, and I contributed stockings for the company, as the Japanese tabi is hardly roomy enough to contain much in the way of Christmas gifts. We hung seven stockings (one for Bruce), and labeled each in English and Japanese, so that Santa Claus could make no mistake. Then we went around the room and put in our parcels, filling up the chinks with oranges, peanuts, cakes, and candy, and placing the overflow on the chairs on which the stockings were hung. We did not finish our job until pretty late in the night, so when I went to bed at last, I slept peacefully until my cook aroused me in the morning, as he came in to make the fire, with a "Merry Christmas," learned especially for the occasion, for he speaks no English at all at other seasons of the year. Then I found that all Miné's family were up and out, and having a grand race around the garden to work off their excitement, for we had agreed to wait until all were ready before any of us went into the parlor. I dressed in a hurry when I found that I was the last, but before I was half ready little Shige was on the stairs shouting "Merry Christmas," and twice before I came down I heard her call up to me in most pathetic tones, "Mada desu ka?"

("not yet?") When at last I was ready, we all went into the parlor together and took down our stockings. My presents were certainly most satisfactory, and as for Bruce, I am sure he never had such a Christmas in his life. Little Shige gave him a big stick, elegantly attired in a pink paper kimono with a crape sash. As soon as it appeared from the depths of Bruce's stocking he gave a yelp of delight, made a dive at it, and after a dance with it around the room, proceeded to undress it, to Shige's great amusement. Beside the stick, the various members of the family had given him a fine ball, a paper of cakes, some candy, and a new collar, all of which he appreciated highly. My presents were a heavy silk obi, the one thing necessary to complete my Japanese costume; a furushiki or bundle handkerchief, of bright colored crape, with my name and address on it in Japanese; a dwarfed flowering plum-tree, all in bud, that will be in bloom in a few days; and a funny Japanese thing that is rather hard to describe, but as it is very characteristic of Japan at this season and seems to form a part of the preparations for the New Year, I must try to make you see it with my eyes. It is a pliant, many-sprayed branch of a tree, and every spray is covered with round balls, pink and white and green and yellow and every imaginable color. Beside these balls, which alone would give it a very gay appearance, there are various objects hanging from the branch. A great white die, made of the same rice flour paste as the balls, swings from a slender thread on one spray; a small, fat, pink and white puppy of the same material dangles from another; a tin Fuji-Yama painted green, a tin coin painted yellow, intended to represent the ancient gold coin of Japan, and numerous other objects, that I can neither describe nor understand, adorn this curious Christmas tree. So far as I have been able to discover, these branches are used simply for decoration, although the adornments have each some symbolical meaning — exactly what, I cannot find out.

When we had finished examining and exclaiming over our stockings, I sent for my servants, and gave them their presents in the shape of cloth for dresses for each. These were received with many profound bows and delighted smiles and a chatter of grateful Japanese, of which I could understand the drift if not all the words. Then we all went off to breakfast, and after breakfast we sent for the children of the cook and the groom. There are eight of them, and they came and stood in a row in the sunny garden, doubling themselves up in the funniest little bows, and with their little black eyes shining and their dirty round faces smiling in a way that was wonderfully attractive. Miné gave them sweets, and I gave each a toy, and they went off radiant, their arms so full that they left a trail of cakes and candies along their line of march, to Bruce's great delight.

At eleven o'clock I went up to the English church at Shiba, the first time I have been to a service in English for a good many weeks. The church was prettily decorated, and I found the service very pleasant, in spite of the fact that I lost my place in the prayer-book, and was compelled to submit to the ignominy of having it found for me again by an English lady, who probably classified me as a heathen or a dissenter, and I hardly know which is the worse in English eyes.

After lunch, our entire household started

off for the Christmas celebration at the native Japanese church that we attend. We found the church quite full, though seats had been kept for us near the front. The decorations were pretty, and there were three big Christmas trees on the platform where the pulpit usually stands. The shutters were closed and the trees brilliantly lighted. The exercises consisted of speeches both by the Sunday-school children and by the grown folks; songs and recitations in Japanese and English; a little dialogue in Japanese between Santa Claus and some of the children; and the distribution of prizes and presents. We sang the carols that we had been practicing for some weeks, and as our audience was not critical they were received with enthusiasm. The whole affair was very pleasant, not so much for what was said, for of course I could understand very little of that, but for the friendly, pleasant, childlike spirit that showed itself everywhere. I do not think I was ever in a church the members of which seemed to be so active and so entirely friendly and united, and it is one of the few places in this country where I feel perfectly at home.

Everywhere else in Japan I feel that I am a foreigner, for though as a rule the Japanese are very kind and polite to foreigners, they place them in the position of outsiders. But in this church it is entirely different; here, "we are no more strangers and foreigners." The spirit of the place seems to be so thoroughly Christian that it is of no age nor race, but of all ages and for all races. It speaks well for Japanese Christianity that this church has grown up and is getting to be a power in Tōkyō with no bolstering or coddling by any missionary board. Its pastor receives a salary of $40 per month, and the whole monthly expense of the church amounts to about $40 more.

January 1, 1889.

To-day all Tōkyō is out in gala costume in honor of the New Year. For several weeks there has been an air of preparation about the city: the shops have been bright with holiday goods and filled with purchasers, and for the last few days the householders have been decorating their house fronts with green, and on almost every street corner little booths have been put up, where pine-trees, bamboo-trees, and rice-straw decorations are sold. Some of the arrangements of pine and bamboo are very pretty, and the streets have a most festive aspect. Miné and I decided to decorate our gate-posts with an arrangement of pine and bamboo that I had noticed and especially fancied, so we sent out my cook, who is also my steward and general purchasing agent, to make inquiries about the price. He came back with information that it would cost $2.50 if we had a gardener put it up, but that he could get the materials and put it up himself for ninety-five cents. We told him to go ahead and do the thing himself, and the result seems, to my unsophisticated eyes, to be all that could be desired.

I believe I have spoken of my cook before. I regard him as quite a wonderful man. He is a remarkably handy person about the house, a fairly good cook, entirely honest, and a Christian. He belongs to the samurai class, is well educated, and reads Chinese poetry for amusement. Imagine a cook in America employing her leisure time over Horace or Virgil!

Last evening, I went down to Ginza, one of the principal business streets of the city, for I had been told that the sights would be well worth the trip. Two of the young girls in our house went with me as escort. They rode together in a double kuruma, while I followed them, drawn by my pet strong man, a perfect Hercules of a kurumaya, who runs as fast as a horse, and drags me along as if I were a mere feather. Our way lay for quite a distance through very dark streets, lighted only by wandering kuruma lanterns, and then suddenly we passed through one of the great gloomy gateways which shut off the different divisions of the city from each other, and there was a street all ablaze with lanterns and torches, and alive with people and booths. Flags were flying from every possible point, long fringes of rice straw were streaming in the wind, and the whole street was aglow with light and color. Through all this brilliancy we traveled for a couple of miles, and it was a sight well worth our long ride in the dark. All through these busy streets there was so great a crowd of merrymakers that the kurumas could hardly be pulled through it, and we had to go very slowly and carefully, our men grunting out warnings as they pushed aside the solid mass ahead of us. But in spite of all their care and their slow pace, the wheel of the forward kuruma became locked with the wheel of a little truck dragged along carelessly by a little gaping man in a long blue gown. For a moment it looked as if there might be an accident, but the wheels were soon disentangled and the double kuruma went on, and I supposed that that adventure was over. Not so Yasaku, my kurumaya. He was resolved to avenge the insult offered to our party upon the head of the stupid little man with the truck, for a kurumaya never forgives an insult to his passenger, and Yasaku is nothing if not brave and truculent. So still holding the shafts with his hands, he gave a little jump like a half-broken colt, and kicked with both legs at the truck that had dared to impede our progress. So well aimed and so forcible was the kick, that the little truck went flying sidewise through the crowd and almost into a booth, and the little man must needs go with it, nearly losing his balance in his swift flight. But even truckmen have feelings, and our little man could not passively submit to being kicked through the crowd. However, as Yasaku was big and he very small, as Yasaku was looking very fierce, white with rage, and chattering like a monkey, while the little truckman himself had the heart of a sick chicken, he followed the safest line of attack, and rushed at my kuruma from behind, giving it a push that almost threw Yasaku down and me out, picked up his truck before the astonished Yasaku could find out what had happened, and made the best of his way into the crowd. At this, Yasaku dropped the shafts and swooped down on his small adversary, looking like a great bird, in his wing-sleeved blouse and his close-fitting dark tights. He seized the little man, and slapped him on the back again and again with the flat of his hand, with such force that the sound was as of a drum. Then Yasaku came back to me, picked up the shafts, and prepared to trot soberly along once more. But the little man had not had enough, it seemed, and came back for more, attacking Yasaku furiously as soon as he saw him occupied once more with his kuruma. But by this time the kurumaya who was drawing the forward kuruma, and who had gone on before the fight began, came back to see what had become of us, and decided that he would take a hand in the row, so he dropped his kuruma, Yasaku once more dropped his, and they gave their small tormentor such a slapping that he at last allowed us to go on, following us with loud but ineffectual vituperations as we proceeded upon our victorious way.

The whole affair was so intensely funny from beginning to end that I could do nothing but laugh, as I sat helpless in my kuruma, now shoved from behind, now dropped down in front, again left entirely alone in the midst of the strange crowd, while the fight raged at a distance. Even had I had complete control of the Japanese language, I could not have produced any impression upon the combatants, for they were too much absorbed in what they were about to notice anything else. Fortunately for our trip that evening, the ever-present police of Tōkyō seemed to be celebrating the New Year in some other portion of the city, for none of them appeared, or our men might have been arrested, leaving us to watch out the old year in Ginza, or else pull our own jinrikishas back with us. I noticed that when we were finally started, our men darted as quickly as possible down the first side street they came to, and made their way discreetly through the darkest streets homeward.

As to-day is New Year's Day, every one in Tōkyō is out in new clothes. All of our family — Miné, her cousin, her girls, and our men-servants, our maid-servants, and our servants' children — are arrayed in garments donned for the first time in honor of the new year. This morning, while I was at breakfast, the cook's three little ones stole on noiseless tabi-shod feet to the door, one at a time, made their little bows, and offered me the New Year's greeting. Pretty little things they are, and very proud of their new kimonos, which they wear with a dignity befitting their newness. Later on my groom came, all rigged out in fine style, and prostrated himself before me, groveling with his head on the floor while he made a series of polite speeches of congratulation. I have not yet become used to this kind of politeness, and I cannot say that I enjoy it very much, but it is expected of servants in this country, and it seems wiser to permit it than to allow them to treat me with less outward respect than they would show to a Japanese employer. It is a curious thing, though, that in spite of all this prostration and groveling before their masters, servants here are on much more easy and friendly terms with their employers than they are in America, and their position is much more independent and responsible. They take out their servility in manners, and retain their real independence in a way that is quite surprising. So far as I am able to judge, personal and domestic service here occupy a much more desirable position among employments than with us.

January 3.

One of the noticeable features of the New Year's season here is the number of street performers who go from house to house, giving a show or a song for a few cents, and reaping a pretty fair harvest of coppers, I should imagine, in a day's work. Two such shows came to us on the afternoon of New Year's Day, and I was glad to have a chance to see what their performance was. The first troupe consisted of two jolly-looking men, going about to exorcise the evil spirits from the houses of their patrons. The exorcism, which is supposed to remain effectual throughout the year, was simply a queer, droning song, accompanied by posturings and grimaces, mostly of a cheerful and mirth-inspiring character. After they had finished their performance, received their small gratuity, and departed, leaving us good luck for the coming year, quite a large company of street musicians strolled into our yard, carrying musical instruments and masks. They gave an entertaining performance, posturing and dancing, changing, by means of masks and a few simple draperies, from demons to women, from women to fearful, red-faced, goggle-eyed beasts, and dancing different dances to suit the various characters that they assumed. Poor Bruce, with staring eyes and bristling hair, bore with these strange transformations as long as the men remained outside of the house, but when one performer, bolder than the rest, came into the front hall personating a much conventionalized lion, Bruce flew at him, growling fiercely, so that he was forced to retreat.

The New Year began with the sharpest earthquake that I have yet experienced.

AN EARTHQUAKE.

I was visiting a sick friend in one of the few large foreign-built houses in our neighborhood. It was terrible to hear the earthquake as it traveled diagonally across the house from corner to corner, shaking everything shakable, including walls and floors, until it seemed as if the house must come down about our ears. We all started for the door, but by the time we reached it the rumbling and shaking stopped. It took my heart some time to recover its normal regularity after the fright, for, somehow, to have the house pitching and rolling like a ship in a storm does set one's heart bobbing about in a most singular manner. My curiosity in regard to earthquakes is now fully satisfied. We have been having them nearly every day lately, but all have been very slight except this one. I have often been awakened in the night by a trembling of the house like the shaking of a steamship from the motion of its screw, but with nothing frightful about it. Bruce usually gets up and looks out of the window when this occurs, I think with a view to finding out whether we are back on shipboard again. But now I know what a good-sized earthquake feels like, and I do not care for any more, large or small.

My friend's little boy, who was asleep in her room when the earthquake occurred, amused us very much, when it was over, by demanding another one immediately. When he found that earthquakes could not be made to meet his order, he insisted on making his New Year's bow to me before he could be induced to resign himself to slumber, so I went over to his bed, and the polite little flannel bundle made me a profound bow, and gave me his New Year's greeting. Then with an easy conscience and his social duties fully performed, he lay down once more, and was soon sound asleep.

January 6.

We had our first snow on Thursday, but it disappeared entirely before Friday night, and now the streets are quite dry, even dusty again. To-day is the coldest day that we have had, with the ground frozen everywhere out of the sun. This is the beginning of the twenty days that the Japanese regard as the coldest season of their winter, and it has been a regular March day, with a high wind blowing; very cold in the wind, but quite warm and comfortable in sheltered spots. On Friday, when the snow lay upon the ground, I sent for a kuruma, and the man made his appearance with feet bare, except for a pair of straw sandals, and his legs covered only by a pair of short blue cotton trousers reaching half way to the knee. He was fairly blue with the cold when he started, but soon warmed up with his work, and seemed comfortable enough. The kurumayas trust to their exercise to keep them warm in winter, and wear the minimum of clothing for the sake of convenience in running. When they stop, they blanket themselves with their lap-robes, which are often of brilliant red. A row of kurumayas waiting for fares, each with his blanket wrapped about him, looks not unlike a company of Indians fresh from the plains. On cold nights, the kurumaya sometimes secures artificial warmth by lighting his lantern and putting it inside his blanket.

CHAPTER VII.

January 13 to 30.

Discharging a Groom. — The New Kurumaya. — The Emperor's Moving-Day. — A New Year's Lunch. — Buying a Kuruma. — A New Horse. — The Japanese Language. — The Promulgation of the Constitution. — Tombs of the Loyal Rōnin.

Tōkyō, January 13, 1889.

Our great excitements last week were in connection with the two extremes of Japanese society. I discharged my groom and succeeded after some difficulty in getting him off the premises, and the Emperor moved from the old barrack of a palace in which he has been living for the last seventeen years, to the new palace just completed, of which I have written you once or twice in these letters.

Perhaps it may not seem to you that discharging one's groom is a very interesting affair, but I can tell you that in this case it became quite exciting before the business was finally ended. The bettōs, as they are called, are regarded as a very unprincipled lot of men, the lowest and most unreliable of all servants. This fellow that I had was sent to me by one of my Japanese friends, who believed him to be more honest than the average, and a skillful and reliable groom. At first I disliked the man, for he seemed inclined to get me to make all sorts of unnecessary purchases for the stable, at higher prices than my cook thought right, but I hauled him up sharply on that, and for a while he seemed to improve. His manners were always attractive, as I think I have written, and he was well built, wore his clothes jauntily, and ran gracefully and well; so though I distrusted him a good deal, and Bruce disliked him heartily, I kept him even after I sold my horse, thinking that it was better to keep him for the new horse, when I should get one, than to run the risk of finding a worse successor. However, idleness was not good for the man; he was off all the time, gambling and drinking, and when he came back a little excited with saké, he would brag to my cook of his iniquities. My cook is, as I have said before, a Christian, and a most upright and moral man, and it seemed to be my bettō's delight to scandalize him by stories of his own sins. One thing the bettō bragged of was that he had three wives living in different parts of the city, but I should not have discharged him for that, as it is quite too common a failing in Japan to be much of an iniquity in a groom. What finally decided me in regard to the man was that one day he confided to the cook how he had taken out my horse and run him in some races that were held near here in November, and had won two blankets with him. He had asked me if he might take the horse to those races, and I had expressly forbidden him, and the performance was not simply taking undue liberties with my property, but was direct disobedience as well. Those races decided his fate, as I concluded that I did not want to keep a servant of that character, and on Christmas Day I told him that, as I had sold my horse, I did not need him any longer, and he could go the first of the year. He took his warning very sweetly, smiled affably, bumped his forehead against the floor a great many times as it was delivered to him, and expressed his respect and regard for me in many words before he backed out of my presence; but he made up for his politeness to me by flying out at my unfortunate cook, whom he scared nearly out of his wits by dire and mysterious threats of vengeance. Cook San seized the earliest opportunity to bring into the house all of my stable property that he could lay his hands on, but when that graceless groom finally moved out on the 10th, he carried with him blankets, curry-combs, brushes, pails, and a variety of small odds and ends, not to speak of the new suit of clothes that I had had made for him, with my monogram embroidered in the middle of the back. He took the opportunity when Miné and the cook were out of the house to come in and bid me an affecting farewell and then decamp, explaining to the cook's wife, when she inquired about the blankets and other things, that if I asked about them he would come and explain why he had taken them. With this mysterious message he departed. When the situation was explained to me, as it was at some length when Miné came back, it struck me as absurd that I should be made such a fool of by a rascally groom. Miné and I pondered the matter until at last, after various conferences with the cook and my new kurumaya, we decided to send a messenger to the address that the groom had left us, with a note politely informing him that he had made a mistake and carried off some of my things. If he did not give them up for the asking, we would then send the police after him. After both Cook San and Yasaku had given excellent reasons why it would not be wise or politic for either of them to go, we secured as messenger a man from a neighboring jinrikisha stand. He departed at about eleven in the morning and returned at four in the afternoon, bringing word that he had scoured the entire district mentioned in the address, but no person of that name was known in the neighborhood. So you see that I was completely fooled by the man, and though the value of the things that he stole from me was not great, I did not enjoy the experience. However, I decided to do nothing more about the matter, as, if I put it into the hands of the police and they did not succeed in catching the thief, he might take his revenge on me by stealing or poisoning my dog. One of the iniquities that the scamp had bragged of to Cook San was that he had killed one of the horses at a stable from which he had been dismissed, and he had expressed a wish to be informed if I should ever get another horse and another groom. I am not at all afraid for my horse, for my big kurumaya whom I have just engaged, and who will sleep in the stable, is both honest and valiant, and would, I am sure, be more than a match for the bettō, should he ever visit my stable with evil intent. My new man is the same Yasaku of whom I have spoken in a previous letter as so very strong and fast. I have been hiring him, when I could get him, from a neighboring jinrikisha stand, but have now taken him altogether into my service, to do double duty as groom and kurumaya. I am delighted to secure so good a servant, for he does three times as much work about the place as the groom ever did, and is always on hand to run errands, carry my books when I go to school, help my visitors' kurumayas up the steep hill that leads to my house, and make himself useful in thousands of ways that the bettō never dreamed of.

Now, having written at some length

about the bettō and his successor, I must tell you about the Mikado's moving-day. Our school was to have begun on Friday, the 11th, but as that was the day fixed upon for the Emperor's removal, the schools were given a holiday in honor of the event. For weeks past, the streets between the old palace and the new have been filled with jovial companies of coolies, carrying on their shoulders in great litters the various imperial household goods. There seems to have been a great deal of rubbish transported in this way, for I have caught glimpses of old furniture, etc., that would hardly strike us as worth the trouble of transporting; but apparently everything that the Emperor has ever used must be moved, even if it be nothing but an empty astral oil-can. Of course, many valuable things have been moved too, but the curious crowd has seen only the rubbish, for the valuables were all carefully boxed, and the boxes covered with great blue or purple cloths, stamped with the white imperial chrysanthemum.

On the night of the 10th, the moving was ended by the removal of the imperial insignia from the old palace to the new, and from that event the Emperor's occupation of his new home will probably be dated. These imperial insignia are to the Emperors of Japan what the crown jewels are to European monarchs; but besides, there is attached to them the religious significance that belongs to the relics of a patron saint. They are the sword, the mirror, and the jewel handed down by Jimmu Tenno, the first Emperor of Japan, to his descendants, and which have passed in turn to each emperor who has reigned in the twenty-five hundred years or more since the great ancestor of the imperial house was called away from the earth. The tradition is that Jimmu Tenno was a son of the gods, and that these sacred objects were given him by the gods themselves, with the prophecy that so long as they should remain in the possession of his descendants the Empire of Japan should endure. Hence the veneration with which they have always been regarded, and the sacredness that attaches to the Emperor and his court as the guardians of these relics. During the Middle Ages, when Japan was almost torn asunder by the wars and rivalries of the great families who aspired to the position of chief adviser to the Emperor, going often so far as to support different scions of the imperial house as rightful heirs to the throne, whichever of the contestants could show that their Mikado was in possession of these treasures established at once, on that ground alone, his right to the titles and the throne. In Japan, so far, it has never occurred to even the most ambitious mind that any one could be received as emperor who was not a lineal descendant of Jimmu Tenno, and who did not have in his possession the imperial insignia; and hence, in the history of Japan, while we find the names of many who have virtually usurped the imperial power, no one has ever made an attempt to usurp the imperial throne; and so, when the insignia were removed on the 10th and placed in their shrine in the penetralia of the new palace, needs must that the Emperor should leave his old abode and follow the sacred symbols of his power to their new resting-place.

As I said, the school was given a holiday on that eventful Friday, but teachers and pupils were told to be on hand at nine o'clock, so as to be ready to stand in line and bow when the Emperor should go by.

Even before nine o'clock, when we went up to school, the street, on both sides, from the Emperor's gate on, was lined with the district school children, each school under command of its teachers, and each carrying white banners. The children looked very pretty, the boys in their Europeanized uniform caps, the girls, almost without exception, in the Japanese costume of purple hakama, or kilt-plaited divided skirt, which forms the uniform of the little school-girls. It was a brisk, cool morning, and, as we came by, one teacher was warming up his class of little ones by some calisthenic exercises, into which they entered with a will.

At about half past nine the bell rang, and our school went out, and drew up in line directly in front of our building. Our children, in their dowdy foreign dresses, were not as pretty in detail as the district school children, but as they are very fond of using a great many bright colors, our line was the gayest of all. The school children stretched in two continuous lines for the mile and a half that lies between the two palaces, making a bright little fence along the road for the whole distance, and they alone were allowed an uninterrupted view of the imperial progress, for all intruders were carefully kept away by the police.

At last, as we stood there stamping our feet to keep them warm, — for the ground was cold and damp, though the sunshine was bright and warm, — a mounted officer came galloping along to make sure that the way was clear. On his heels came the imperial guard, their red and white pennants fluttering gayly and their horses dancing friskily. Then followed the Emperor's carriage, with its red hangings and black, white, and gold liveried lackeys. As the carriage came out of the court gate, the children at the end of the line began the Japanese national air, and the wild, martial, and inspiring music was carried along the line as fast as the coach moved, so that all the way to the palace the Emperor was accompanied by the children's voices. It was a pretty idea, I thought, and the voices sounded sweetly in the open air, their queer metallic tone suiting the Japanese music much better than it does the foreign. After the Emperor's coach came another mounted body-guard, and then the Empress and her ladies, in a coach exactly like the Emperor's. Of course we had to bow as the coaches went by, and we did not see the Emperor and Empress at all, but I did not care very much, as I had seen the Emperor and examined him carefully, and I am likely to have a good many opportunities to see the Empress before the year is ended. A long line of carriages, containing the rest of the imperial household, followed, and then the show was over, and we were allowed to go home. I am sure the children must have been glad to be marched off singing, under their teachers' lead, for many of them had been standing in line for an hour and a half.

Yesterday, school assembled, but there were no lessons. We met in the gymnasium to hear speeches from the president, the lady principal, and some of the directors of the school. After they were over, the girls were dismissed, but the teachers remained to a lunch, where the ceremonial New Year's dishes were served. It was rather the least attractive lunch that I have ever been called upon to eat, for the dishes are historic, and belong to a former period, and are not much relished even by the Japanese of the present day. There was saké, which I do not like any better than any other kind of wine, and therefore do not drink; and soup, containing large, rank-flavored mushrooms and greens of some kind; and cuttlefish, both dried and stewed. I tried some of the dried cuttlefish, and found that in the mouth it is difficult to distinguish from a leather shoe-string, but I did not attempt the stewed variety, as Miné assured me that she did not like it. Beside these things, there were various kinds of raw fish, cut into thin slices and served with pickled chrysanthemums, horse-radish, sea-weed, and shōyu. I managed to eat quite a good deal of the raw fish, which is really not bad after you have pocketed your prejudices, and if you flavor it up well with the condiments. I was pleased to see that, though there were three foreigners at the table beside myself, and all have been in Japan much longer than I have, I could eat the Japanese food more easily, and manage the chopsticks better, than any of them, thanks to the cosy Japanese lunches that I have taken with my friends in their own homes. I have come to the conclusion that there are very few foreigners in Japan who have my opportunities, and I trust I am duly thankful, and shall make good use of them. Foreigners may live in Japan for years and not see so much of real Japanese life as I have been able to see in the few months since I began housekeeping in Tōkyō.

January 25.

I have just bought a kuruma, or, rather, had one built, for the regular Japanese size is a pretty tight fit for me. The whole cost of it, finished, and with my monogram painted on the lacquered panel at the back, was nineteen yen. My kurumaya wears the same monogram embroidered on his coat, right between the shoulders, and the paper lantern that he carries at night is decorated in the same way, so that even after dark the outfit can be picked out of a crowd of others as belonging to me. I feel very fine as I ride about the city in my new equipage, and it is a great comfort to have a pleasant, strong man always at hand to take me anywhere at a moment's notice.

I am at present trying horses again. I have found two that I like, and am divided in my mind between them. I have a strong leaning toward a pretty and intelligent little black beast, with a good deal of spirit and delightfully easy gaits, but I am afraid that he is too small and too young for me. The one that I think I ought to buy is a heavier and stronger gray, with an obstinate carriage of the head, and a dangerous pair of heels. Japanese ponies are rarely good-natured, and are always looking for a chance to kick, bite, or strike out with their forefeet, and as the little black seems to have a good temper, and the gray is one of the kind that cannot be trusted, I am tempted to buy the black for his moral qualities.

January 30.

I bought a horse yesterday, and am much pleased with my purchase. I finally yielded to the charms of the little black. My cook and kurumaya, who are to divide the care of him, are also pleased with the addition to the family. He certainly seems more of a horse and less of a machine than Dawn, in whom I could never get up the slightest interest.

I really feel that I am getting to know something about the language, under

Miné's efficient instruction. I find that
after every lesson the next one is learned
more easily, and, although I know very
little yet, I feel considerably encouraged. I
think it is broadening to the mind to study
a language that is so altogether different
from all past experiences in that line.
Imagine a language that contains only
three parts of speech, the noun, the verb,
and the adjective, and in which any one
word may be all three, so that if you hear
a word that you may happen to be familiar
with as a noun, you cannot tell whether it
is behaving like a noun on this particular occasion, or whether it is not doing
the work of a verb or an adjective. I am
beginning to understand a great many of
the apparently stupid mistakes that my
pupils make in English, as I see what an
absolutely fluid thing their native tongue is.
As for grammar, there is none to speak
of, since there is really almost nothing to
classify, words slide around in such a way
from one kind of work to another. In the
written language I am not making much
progress. I am still laboring with the
kata kana, but I know that pretty well now,
and mean to take up the hira kana next

week. The letters are terribly slippery, and one of the great difficulties in retaining them in the mind lies in the fact that, after they are pretty well learned, there is almost no opportunity to practice reading with them, for of course, with so many letters and characters as are used here, you may go for days without seeing anything in which the particular ones that you have just learned occur. Fortunately, I was given a little magazine the other day, in which there is a long article written entirely in kata kana, and now I practice reading aloud from it, a task that is much more encouraging than hunting out what I do know from a wilderness of hieroglyphics that I do not know at all. Without that little magazine, I am sure I should have given up the letters in despair.

Japan is in quite a state of expectation over the near approach of the day set for the promulgation of the Constitution. The day fixed for the ceremony is February 11, the anniversary of the accession of Jimmu Tenno to the throne, 660 B. C. All the most learned men of Japan, together with various foreign lawyers, imported by the government at great expense, have been at work on the Constitution for years, and now it is to be promulgated, so that the people will have a year to study it before it goes into force. There is to be some kind of a grand ceremonial connected with the event, but I shall not be able to see it, as it is only for the high officials, who will be gathered together in the palace on that day from the whole empire.

I had a delightful ride the other day with a Japanese friend. We went out to the tombs of the forty-seven rōnins, and I found the place very impressive. In the temple near which they are buried are kept the relics of the faithful servants, — swords, armor, etc.; but those are only shown on certain days, and we were there on the wrong day. The gravestones form a hollow square, and are shut off from the other graves in the cemetery by a fence. The inclosure is hard by the great stone block that marks the resting-place of the lord, to avenge whose death the faithful servants died. Before each gravestone incense is always burning, and has been for the two hundred years since the graves were made, — supplied during all this time by the offerings of visitors to the tomb, so sacred is loyalty in the minds of the Japanese! The place is densely shaded, and the fragrant smoke hangs low under the trees, making the air thick and heavy throughout the inclosure. Forty-eight men are buried there, and the story of the forty-eighth is this: A Satsuma man insulted the leader of the rōnins for not avenging the death of his lord, at a time when, for the sake of disarming suspicion, the whole band had scattered, and the leader was living a most dissolute and apparently purposeless life. This Satsuma man, when he heard of the long waiting and the bold stroke by which the death was at last avenged, was overcome with remorse as he thought of the undeserved insult that he had inflicted, and to prove the sincerity of his repentance, he committed hara-kiri upon the tomb of the leader, and was buried with the faithful forty-seven.

CHAPTER VIII.

FEBRUARY 12 TO 20.

The Promulgation Festival. — Morning Scenes on Koji-machi. — Exercises at the School. — Imperial Progress through Tōkyō Streets. — Evening Rides and Street Sights. — Rice and Eels. — Mingling with the Holiday Crowd. — Murder of Viscount Mori. — Viscount Mori's Funeral. — Religious Liberty under the Constitution. — Another Earthquake.

Tōkyō, February 12, 1889.

YESTERDAY morning, when I awoke, the snow lay thickly over everything, and was still falling, so that there seemed no possibility of the great public rejoicings that had been planned to celebrate the promulgation of the Constitution. However, in spite of the snow, we heard a tum-tumming on the business street above us that led us to believe that some one was doing something in honor of the day, and after much persuasion I succeeded in inducing Miné to put on her worst clothes and arctics, and we sallied out in the snow and slush to see what might be going on.

When we reached Kojimachi, the business street before referred to, the sight was most melancholy. The night before, as Yasaku brought me home through it, it had been gay with flags and lanterns, but now, all the decorations that could be taken down had disappeared, and nothing remained to do honor to the day except a few moist, depressed, and wretched-looking flags. Here and there people were wandering disconsolately about, muddy nearly up to their waists, and the scene was anything but festive; still, in the distance we heard the beating of drums, so we splashed along the street to find out, if we could, who it was that was cheerful under such depressing circumstances. On our way we passed a mournful spectacle. Some enterprising householders had put all their small savings together, and had erected two enormous flags on bamboo poles, the poles crossing over the street and tied together with a huge bow-knot of purple silk cord with tassels hanging from it. The night before, the flags had formed one of the most imposing decorations on all the long, bright street. But unfortunately they were not dyed to meet such weather, and the red from the sun in the centre of each flag had spread itself out over the white ground, changing it to a dirty pink, while the snow beneath was grewsome with the gory rain that had dripped from the demoralized banners. Every one who came by stopped to utter some exclamation of pity for the poor people whose efforts to decorate were thus ruined. A little way beyond this wreck we found the place from which the alluring sounds proceeded. We stopped in front of a small house, which would have been a shop on any other day, and there was a big two-story cake set in a sort of shrine, with candles in front of it, and a number of men seated on the floor beside it beating drums and blowing on flutes, while a little crowd was standing in the slushy street listening to the somewhat inharmonious din. I have not yet been able to discover what it was all about, but it cheered us somewhat to feel that some one was celebrating even in this incomprehensible way. After we had seen that, we thought we were cold and wet and muddy enough to go home, which we accordingly did, sure that there would be nothing more to see on that day.

As we were sitting in my parlor after our return, we heard the salute which announced that the ceremony in the palace was over, and that the Constitution had been given by the Emperor to his ministers. At that very moment the clouds began to break, and soon the sun was shining, but still, when I started for school at a little before twelve, I had no idea that there would be any review, for the roads were in a terrible condition with slush and mud. But when I reached the top of the hill I saw squads of soldiers marching out to the parade ground, officers riding back and forth, flags flying, lanterns being hung up as fast as possible, and all the signs of preparation for the great event. Miné had gone to school a little before me, and when I reached there I found that the teachers were engaged in bowing to the Emperor's picture, a ceremony which is fortunately not required of foreigners. I am afraid that I could not bring myself to do it, for I think it is of the nature of an act of worship; at any rate, it is too much like that for me to want to perform it. The Emperor's picture is kept in a room that is only opened for this ceremony, or for the

Empress when she visits the school. The teachers high enough in rank to be received at court are not expected to bow before the picture, but all of the others must do so on special occasions, such as the Emperor's birthday, New Year's Day, etc. When the teachers had finished, the pupils were brought up in classes and put through, and then we went to our chilly assembly room, and there was some koto and piano music, and some fuzzy singing by the girls. After these exercises were over, we put on our wraps, and went out and stood in line for an hour in front of the building, and watched the funny Japanese crowd until the procession came by. Upon this occasion, for the first time, the Emperor and Empress rode in the same coach, and it is really a great step up, so far as the women of the country are concerned. The theory hitherto has been that the Emperor is too far above his wife in dignity to appear in public with her in the same carriage, but yesterday, by riding with her, he recognized the fact that his wife is raised by her marriage to his own social level. It is a formal adoption of the Western idea in regard to the position of the wife.

The procession was the finest that I have seen yet. First there were the mounted, gold-laced soldiers, carrying red and white pennons, who always march in front of the Emperor's carriage. These were followed by four or five state coaches, containing the princes and cabinet ministers. Then came another squad of horsemen, and then the most gorgeous coach that I have ever seen, drawn by six black horses, each led by a magnificent black, white, and gold liveried groom, while the coachman on the box was so bedizened with gold that he looked like a lay figure rather than a real man. Just at this point we all bowed, so that I saw nothing more but the top of the Empress' bonnet as she turned to look at her little peeresses, who seem to have a warm place in her heart. When we lifted our heads, the splendid vision was gone, and there was nothing more to see except every-day black carriages, which seemed very tame after the state coaches. After the procession proper had passed, there came an indiscriminate medley of things that had been accumulating behind the detachment of police who had kept the road clear. The dam once removed, they swept down upon us like a flood: the populace in all degrees of mud and jollity; big-bugs with gold lace in kurumas; bigger bugs with more gold lace in carriages; horsemen, foot-soldiers, artillery, — all in one grand mêlée. Why nobody was walked on by the horses or run over by the gun-carriages I do not at all understand, but nobody was, at least in our neighborhood. We were very glad to get out of the crowd and back into the schoolhouse, for beside the danger we were in of being trampled on, our feet were numb from standing so long on ground that had been covered with snow only an hour or two before. We remained at school long enough to receive notice of a holiday the next day, and then came home, but went out again as soon as we had finished dinner, to see what we could of the illuminations. We did not try to go to the places where the decorations were finest, but made a complete circuit of the palace grounds, and enjoyed very much the alternations of moonlight, lantern light, electric light, and gaslight that our ride gave us. When we came into the great open space in front of the palace, a space which was almost as light as day with the electric lights, the invited guests were just going in to the Emperor's reception, and everything was very gay. Fireworks were being set off somewhere on the palace grounds, and fine ones they were, too, so that when we reached home we thought that we had had a very good time, though by avoiding the crowd we had also avoided the best of the show.

February 15.

My last letter took up simply the festivities of Monday, but all day Tuesday the city kept holiday as well. The Emperor made stately progress through another part of the city, and those who had not had a chance to see him the day before might get front places this time. I remained indoors, except for a short horseback ride, until evening, when I joined Miné at the house of her married sister, who lives close to the business part of the town, to take supper there, and then go out to mix with the crowd and see what was going on. I reached there just after dark, and my friends insisted that I should go out at once in my kuruma and ride along the principal thoroughfare to Nihombashi, one of the great bridges of the city. This street was the finest show that I have seen yet. It was spanned by a succession of magnificent green arches, no two alike, set with electric lights, hung with strings of red and white lanterns, decorated with the imperial chrysanthemum, or with great Chinese letters made entirely of small oranges set into the green of the arch. Under these arches surged the crowd of holiday-makers in their best clothes, — men, women, and children, with open mouths and upturned faces, trying to look all ways at once. The buildings on both sides of the street were hung with festoons of flags and lanterns from foundation to roof, and their wide, open fronts were brightly lighted, showing æsthetic backgrounds of screens, brought out from storehouses for the occasion, and which completely hid the ordinary stock-in-trade, turning the shops, for the time being, into dainty little parlors. Upon the floors, which were, in many cases, covered with scarlet blankets, sat the shop-keepers and their families, often entertaining parties of friends with tea and cake in pretty dishes. These interiors, with their brightness and their suggestions of pleasant social life, added a final charm to a scene that was more like dreamland than like reality, and I had to keep punching myself to make myself believe that I was really awake and in my right mind. I went on in my kuruma as far as I dared (there were five miles of just this kind of thing), but I had to come back before seeing it all, for I was afraid that my friends would be waiting supper for me. I found, however, that, owing to the rush of business that night, the eels and rice that had been ordered from an eel-shop close by had not yet arrived. At last, just as we had become so hungry that we were trying to satisfy our appetites on rice and sea-weed, the eels made their appearance, delicately broiled, and laid upon mounds of rice in square, lacquered boxes, one box for each person, and a pair of chopsticks with each box. For a few moments the chopsticks flew at a rapid rate, for we were all very hungry, and all in a hurry to be out in the street. Supper ended, we sallied forth, this time on foot, a party of six, although we soon lost half our number in the crowd, and only found them again as we were coming home. We wandered slowly down the street, just in the opposite direction from the way I had gone before supper, stopping where the crowd was thickest to see what they were looking at, and then walking on again. If you people in America could have been transported to Tōkyō that night and have seen things as we saw them, and nothing more of Japan, you would never have believed that it was anything but an agreeable freak of your imaginations, there was such an atmosphere of unreality and staginess about the whole thing. The city seemed to be wild with rejoicing, and to be showing it in the tasteful, dainty, quiet ways in which the Japanese excel.

But during these two days of festival a tragedy was also enacted, and on the day on which Japan gained a Constitution she lost one of her most enlightened and liberal-minded statesmen. I am going to write out all the details as I had them directly from the lips of one of the cabinet ministers, for I suppose many reports of the affair will reach America, and it may be interpreted as a sign of a reactionary tendency and an outbreak of mediævalism, and I do not think that it can really be attributed to that. The facts, as they are at present known to the authorities, are these, and I give them as I heard them, on the morning of Viscount Mori's death.

On Monday, February 11, as Viscount Mori was dressing to go to the palace for the promulgation ceremony, a man came to the door of his official residence and asked to see the viscount. The servant replied that his master was engaged and could see no one, but that if the man would wait a moment he could see Viscount Mori's private secretary and state his business to him. When the private secretary appeared, the man at first refused to explain his business, but at last said that he had just heard of a plot to assassinate Mr. Mori, and had come to tell him of it, but that he could disclose the details to no one except the minister himself. More than this the secretary could not get out of him, and just then Viscount Mori himself came down the long hall, on his way to his carriage. As he passed, the secretary said to him, "This is the man who wanted to see you." Mr. Mori stopped for a moment, the man stepped forward, and before any of the bystanders could see what he was about, he drew a long, sharp knife from his clothing with his left hand, while with his right he seized Mr. Mori, and then, with a quick movement, plunged the knife into the minister's right side. He had not had time to pull out the knife and strike again when the servants pulled him off, but he broke away from them, and was at once cut down and killed by the sword of a policeman who came in from his station at the gate, as he heard the noise of the struggle. The knife was a common kitchen knife, such as is used by the Japanese for cutting up fish, and it was driven so deep into the minister's side that the handle came off as the murderer tried to pull it out.

Viscount Mori was not rendered unconscious by his wound, and messengers were at once dispatched for doctors, but all the great physicians had gone to court, and all the little ones were out enjoying the holiday, and it was three hours before medical aid could be obtained. During that time the poor man had lost so much blood that, although the wound was not of such a nature as to be necessarily fatal, he died within twenty-four hours. It was about eight, on the morning of the 11th, when the assassin made his fatal call, and Mr. Mori died at eight on the morning of the 12th. His death was not announced until 11.30 that evening, that the festivities of the day might not be interfered with; for here in Japan a man cannot die legally, whatever his condition may be actually, until the government gives him permission. Accordingly, though Viscount Mori drew his last breath early in the morning, the official announcement is that he died at 11.30 at night.

And now as to the reasons for the murder. A paper was found upon the body of the assassin, saying that the viscount had been killed because of sacrilege committed by him the year before at the shrines of Isé. It appears that the minister had visited these, the most sacred of Shinto shrines, and when there had failed to make the customary offerings, had refused to take off his boots before entering the sanctuary, and is said to have even pushed aside the curtain that concealed the sacred treasures. Many conservative Japanese of the lower classes were much worried by this, and were afraid that the protection of the national gods might be withdrawn from a government in which so godless a person was prominent; and the sacrilege so rankled in the heart of this man, who was a humble employee of the government, that he resolved to rid the country of its perpetrator, that the protection of the guardian spirits might not be withdrawn upon the change to a new form of government. The man appears to have been just as much of a crank as Guiteau. He seems to have been entirely alone, and without accomplices. He undoubtedly committed the act from patriotic and religious motives, and not from a mere grudge, but he does not, so far as I can find out, represent any public sentiment, nor is any portion of the population pleased that his patriotism and religion should have taken such a form. It is a misfortune that he should have been killed on the spot instead of having to take his trial, for such summary justice often excites sympathy, when a legal trial and condemnation does not, and in a trial much could have been found out about the man which now will never be known.

February 20.

Mr. Mori's funeral took place on Saturday, but I could not go, as I had an engagement to speak before a ladies' society that afternoon, and could not get it postponed. I did have time, however, to go to a point not far from my house and watch the funeral procession. It was very long and imposing, — infantry, cavalry, and artillery, cabinet ministers in carriages, students from the University and high schools on foot, and a great number of lesser persons in kurumas. Mr. Mori had a strong objection to the extravagance connected with Japanese funeral customs, and every effort was made to have all things simple and as he would have wished. The money sent to his family by the Emperor and Empress and the gifts of others as well are to be used to endow a scholarship in the University, instead of for the purchase of flowers, cakes, etc. While I am on this subject, it may interest you to hear that a reaction in regard to this particular kind of extravagance has set in, and that the Kunaisho (Imperial Household Department) employees, from the greatest to the least, have signed an agreement that they will neither send to funerals of others any gifts, unless they be of money, nor will they undertake to send out from the afflicted house cakes and rice on the fiftieth day after the death, as has been the custom hitherto. This seems to be a step in the right direction, and beginning as it does at the upper end of society, may be followed by others the more easily.

I was visiting one of my Japanese friends the other morning, when her husband, a man of prominent position in the government, came in, bringing the official English translation of the Constitution. With the greatest pride he pointed out to me the twenty-eighth article, which guarantees religious liberty to all Japanese subjects. The article reads as follows: "Japanese subjects shall within limits not prejudicial to peace and order, and not antagonistic to their duties as subjects, enjoy freedom of religious belief."

We had quite an earthquake a few days ago. I am told that it is the most severe shake that Tōkyō has experienced since 1854, although from my own judgment I should not have thought it so severe as the one of New Year's night, of which I wrote you. This most recent one occurred at six o'clock in the morning, when I was still in bed. The house swayed and rocked quite like a ship at sea for several minutes, and I had some thought of trying to get out of doors; but the recollection that my double front doors were tightly bolted, and that before I could get them open it was probable either that the house would fall, or that the shake would be over, served to make me stay quietly where I was. My own house is not nearly so frightful in an earthquake as some of the larger and more solidly built residences, nor so dangerous either, for while my house is built with walls and windows after the foreign style, the posts that support the structure are fitted after the Japanese manner upon rounded stones, and the whole edifice will stand a good deal of shaking without worse damage than breakage of glass in the windows.

CHAPTER IX.

March 1 to 9.

The Wily Bettō. — Yasaku's Domestic Affairs. — Marriage and Divorce. — Developments in Regard to the Mori Murder. — Letters from Nishino to his Family. — A Spring Jaunt. — Toy Collecting.

Tōkyō, March 1, 1889.

Some time ago I wrote you all about my experience in connection with getting rid of my bettō, and how he carried off most of my stable furniture, leaving a false address. I thought that the man would never have the face to appear on my premises again, but I little knew of what effrontery he was capable. He went off, as I told you, leaving word that he would like to know if I ever bought another horse and engaged another bettō, but of course I did not take any pains to keep him informed in regard to my establishment, so he set to work to find out about things for himself.

Not very long ago I received a note from an English lady with whom I am very slightly acquainted, recommending some bettō or other, and saying that although she did not know that I was wanting a bettō, her own groom told her that I did, so she sent the recommendation. I simply sent back word that I was not in need of a groom, and thought no more about it, but I now think that my former employee had resorted to this device for gaining information about me.

A few nights ago, Miné and I went out to dinner, taking Yasaku with us. No sooner were we all safely out of the house than my old bettō walked into the kitchen and made a long call upon my cook. His object in calling seemed to be to establish a claim against Yasaku (who now adds the duties of bettō to those of kurumaya) for six yen, apparently because Yasaku occupies the place from which the old bettō was dismissed. Cook San seized the occasion to make inquiries about the blankets, brushes, etc., that the man had taken away with him, and the groom explained that he had taken them by mistake, and would bring them back the next time he called, — a story that made the cook's eyes twinkle considerably as he told it to us.

It seems that the bettō is still negotiating with Yasaku, through one of his friends, for a money payment for the privilege of occupying the place that the former groom was put out of; and what is to me most mysterious is that Yasaku seems to recognize a claim of some kind, and instead of refusing, is simply trying to see how much he can beat the man down. Miné and I tell him that it is foolish for him to take the matter into consideration at all, but Miné thinks that he will finally pay something.

Yasaku's domestic affairs amuse us very much. When I engaged him, he said that he had a wife at Utsu-no-miya, and that he would send for her to come to Tōkyō, that she might guard the stable when he was out with the kuruma. We have been wondering why his wife did not come, but the other day it came out that there had been a division in the family. Yasaku had written to his wife to come, but the woman had sent back word that she had work now at Utsu-no-miya, and did not want to come at present. Thereupon Yasaku replied that if she could not come now, she need not come at all. This message did not move her, so he divorced her, and is now on the lookout for another and a more dutiful helpmeet. He thought of taking Miné's cook, an exceedingly green and stupid country girl, but concluded that it might inconvenience Miné to have her cook taken away, and for that reason gave her up. Then he began negotiating for some one else, but that fell through, and now he is simply on the lookout in a general way, with a view to making a satisfactory business arrangement.

The whole matter of marriage out here seems to be entirely cold-blooded and devoid of sentiment, though in the higher classes it is a trifle more complicated on account of etiquette than in Yasaku's case. This is simply an instance of what may happen at any time in any family, and be thought very little of. If there are children, they belong to the father, and may be disposed of as he likes, the poor mother having no rights over her children, no matter what the cause of divorce.

Almost every day something more appears in the papers in regard to the Mori murder.

The following clipping from the "Japan Mail" of February 27, containing the last letters written by the murderer, Nishino Buntaro, to his parents and brother and sister, gives an insight into the Japanese mind that seems to me helpful in understanding the people: —

The vernacular press publishes the text of a letter written by Nishino Buntaro, the assassin of Viscount Mori, three days before the perpetration of the deed and his own death. The letter is addressed to Nishino's father. It was intrusted to a friend of the writer for direct delivery or dispatch, — the distinction is not drawn by the Tōkyō journals, — and through this friend's agency it ultimately came into the hands of the newspapers. The letter, literally translated, runs thus : —

"I write to say that my act in killing a Minister of State is not the outcome of a sudden resolve. I planned it when I was at Tokushima last year. For this reason the visit I paid to my home at the fall of last year was solely for the purpose of bidding you farewell. As, however, it was impossible to be assured of facts without examining into them at the place itself of their occurrence, I went to the Shrine Daijin-gu on my way to Tōkyō, and having ascertained by inquiry that things were undoubtedly as represented, I made up my mind to what is now about to happen. You have often told me that the duty of a man is to die before his lord. Thus, though the world, for aught I know, may say that the manner of my death was that of a lunatic, my own feeling is that it will be as that of one who fell on the battlefield before his lord. I pray you, therefore, not to grieve for me. It pains me to think that after having been for more than twenty years the object of your kindness, I should die without testifying my gratitude. Were I your only child, there would be no help. But you have my brother, Nobusuke, and my sister, Michi, and in them I hope you will find consolation. I beg you to make arrangements so that Nobusuke may succeed to the headship of the family, and with a thousand prayers for your happiness, I bid you farewell."

To his mother Nishino wrote as follows: —

"When you hear of what is now about to happen to me, you will doubtless be shocked. But in truth my resolve is of old standing, and the short visit I recently paid you was for the purpose of bidding you farewell. It was for this reason that I had such difficulty in leaving you, and that I could scarcely restrain my tears. I have observed that parents who lose their children forget their own suffering and misfortune, and have pity only for the dead child. And certainly those who die of sickness, or owing to some unexpected catastrophe, are to be pitied in that their death is not of their own seeking. But I die of deliberate choice. I meet my end with just such feelings of pleasure as a man experiences when he goes to a feast. Do not grieve for me, therefore, in the least. Had I been lost at sea on my way to Tōkyō the other day, or had I died of kakke the year before last, there would have been no help, would there? What men will say of me I know not, but since I die believing that it is for the sake of my Sovereign and my country, if you suffer yourself to become broken down with grief, you will only show want of spirit. I pray you, when I am gone, to bestow your care on Nobusuke and Michi in my stead, and thus I bid you farewell."

To his brother and sister, both younger than himself, he also addressed the following letter:

"I am sure that you continue to be always dutiful to your parents and diligent at your studies. I intrust our father and mother to your care after I, your brother Buntaro, am dead. Never forget, I pray you, that you are children of the house of Nishino and people of the Empire of Japan. If you remember unfailingly that you are children of the house of Nishino, the instinct of filial obedience will come to you of its own accord; if you do not forget that you are of the people of the Empire of Japan, loyalty and patriotism will be with you of themselves."

Nishino wrote also to the friend to whose care he intrusted the above letters for delivery to his family. The name of this friend is not published, but the letter addressed to him was as follows: —

"After my visit to Tokushima last summer, the events of the time dwelt much in my thoughts, and since my return to Tōkyō, on the 8th of January, I have seen nothing of you. I am now about to kill Mori, Minister of State. If I succeed, I shall not regret to die. And even though the misfortune of failing to achieve my purpose overtake me, I believe that I shall not die a dog's death; for some one will surely be inspired to prosecute my aim. Succeed or fail, I shall at least have done something towards correcting the degenerate spirit of the people of the country of the gods. It will be as though I fell on the battlefield before my lord's charger. I pray you to take heed for me, so that after I am dead men may know that Buntaro was not mad.

"P. S. Let me entreat you to send the accompanying letters to my father, mother, brother, and sister, after I am dead. I have intrusted them to one or two other persons also, lest through fear of suspicion they might not be forwarded to my parents."

There is now, it seems, a good deal of approval expressed in private for the spirit that prompted the murder, though few go so far as to approve of the murder itself. Old Mr. Nishino, the father of the assassin, receives many letters of condolence, in which his son is not in the least condemned.

It is now said that Mr. Mori did not commit the sacrilege of which he was at first accused, but simply pushed aside the temple curtain with his cane, and when reproved by the priest, bowed and withdrew. His sacrilege, according to the latest reports, consisted in being a little angry at the priest who reproved him, and in not visiting the shrines again during his stay in the neighborhood, nor making the customary offerings for the support of the temples.

March 9.

The last few days have been delightfully warm and bright, so much so that one really began to think of white dresses and that sort of thing, but to-day is rainy, and, though not exactly cold, is colder than it has been. The only drawback to the pleasant weather has been that the inhabitants have regarded it as a sign of impending earthquakes or volcanic disturbances, and so I have gone to bed every night wondering whether my house would tumble about my ears before morning, or whether

I might not be buried under a shower of mud or lava from some hitherto unsuspected volcanic blow-hole. Since feeling one or two lively earthquakes and hearing all about Bandai San, I do not feel as if this were a very certain kind of a country to live in.

Last Wednesday, Miné and I went off on a little expedition together. I think I wrote some time ago that the plums were in bloom in sheltered places. They began early in February, and are now about at their prettiest. Our garden has some fine trees in it, and we enjoy them very much, but there are public gardens in Tōkyō to which all the world goes to see the plum blossoms at their finest, and we decided to visit one of these for a sight not only of the plums, but of the people. My kurumaya was laid up with an attack of indigestion, so we went in a double kuruma with two men tandem. It is the first time that I have ever ridden with any one in a kuruma, and although it is rather close quarters, particularly in thick winter ulsters, it is great fun to have some one to talk with and ask about all the funny street sights, and I enjoyed the ride, which was a very long one, immensely. Our kuruma at last put us down in front of a temple, and we got out to follow the crowd, who had come for the same purpose as ourselves. We did not go into the temple itself, but walked about the grounds, which are notable chiefly for some queer sacred images of animals, and a magnificent wistaria vine which will be worth going to visit in a month or two. Our guide, the crowd, took us out through a gate at the side of the temple inclosure, and we found ourselves on a country road with ugly, black, mud-covered fields on each side. In one of these fields a man was standing up to his waist in mire, turning over the soft, slimy mud with a small, wooden tub. Miné said he was searching for lotus roots, which are quite prized as an article of food here. Farming in Japan is extremely dirty work. Much of it is done under water, and done literally by hand, whole fields being clawed and pawed over with no other tools than the fingers.

But this is a digression. We had to walk quite a distance over this country road, but at last turned down a little lane, and soon found ourselves in a garden planted entirely with plum-trees. The trees were so trained as to be all branches, with no trunks at all, and were so very old that their bark was quite covered with mosses. The tender young blossoms are regarded by the æsthetic Japanese as much more beautiful when they grow upon a venerable, moss-covered tree. The garden was crowded with visitors, from the jinrikisha man in blue blouse and with symmetrical, bare, brown legs, to the fine lady in paint and powder, silk and crape, pattering along on her high, lacquered clogs. All were gazing at the flowers, and seemed lost in admiration. In the centre of the garden grew the finest of the trees, and upon their branches were hung bits of paper on which their admirers had inscribed poems. One tree had ten poems hanging from it, although it was not the one I should have chosen as my favorite, while the tree that I admired the most had not a single poetical offering upon its branches. The crowd eddied and whirled about the decorated trees, stopping to read the various poems, and making temporary blockades. We sat down on a bench under a tree, and an old man brought us tea, and then, when we had watched a youth inditing a poem hard by, we moved on to make room for others. Farther on is another plum garden which we visited, but it was not as interesting as the first, as the trees were not as old, and there were no poems on their branches. On our walk back, we stopped at a little wayside tea-house and took tea and sembei, a sort of toasted rice cracker which is very good, only rather choky. When we reached our kurumas again, we thought we had time to go to Asakusa on our way home. I had not been there since I went last summer in doing the sights of Tōkyō. When we had come as near to the temple as the kurumas were allowed to approach, we got out to walk the rest of the way; but we had to pass a line of small shops, in which every conceivable variety of toy is kept, and so attractive was the display that we succumbed to the temptation, spent all our time at the toy-shops, and did not reach the temple at all.

I have made up my mind that if I undertake a collection of any kind while I am out here, it will be of toys. I think that in a complete collection of the toy tools, implements, furnishings, etc., one could bring home the largest possible amount of the every-day life of Japan, and with the least possible expenditure of money. I have begun with a ceremonial tea service, a box of carpenter's tools, and a small kitchen. This last is the most perfect little thing that you can imagine, — a Japanese kitchen, with all its fittings and utensils, even to the knives and skimmers, the dust-pan, the matches, and the god-shelf. It is now before my eyes as I write, and you might suppose you were looking into a kitchen through the wrong end of an opera-glass, for there are no shams about it; everything is made as carefully as if for use.

CHAPTER X.

March 21 to 31.

A Sad Holiday. — Japanese Mourning Customs. — A Shintō Funeral. — An Earthquake. — Yasaku's Wedding. — Questions on John's Gospel.

Tōkyō, March 21, 1889.

Yesterday was a holiday, but not a very cheerful one, as it was given to us on account of the funeral of one of our girls who died on Monday. She was one of our best scholars in English. Miné was particularly fond of her, and spent much of her time at the house of mourning on Monday, doing what she could to comfort the parents, to whom the end had been a complete surprise. The doctor had cheered them with false hopes, although he had known for some time that there was no chance of recovery, and for several days that the end was near. This Japanese custom of always saying what you think would be agreeable to people, instead of speaking the truth, softens some things, but simply aggravates others, and in this case it could hardly be called a kindness.

I have been much interested in what I have learned during the last few days of Japanese mourning and funeral customs. It seems that when there is a death in a Japanese family where the old customs still prevail, all the friends of the family call at once, and they must be received by the mourners themselves. In this case, the parents of the dead girl, instead of being allowed to sit quietly in some secluded part of the house while an intimate friend of the family received callers and answered inquiries, were obliged to remain all day long by the side of their dead daughter, and there receive all the visits of condolence, and answer all the questions themselves, on pain of being considered impolite if they delegated the task to some one else. Then, after this wearisome day, at nine o'clock in the evening, all the family and the near friends of the deceased were assembled in the room, while the body was placed in the coffin. The coffin is quite a large structure of white wood, room being made in it for many things beside the body itself. All the little things that the young girl had treasured in life were laid with her in the coffin, and, in addition to these, many packages done up in white paper, the contents of which I do not know. Then the coffin was closed, not to be opened again, amid the weeping of those assembled for this last look at the face of their loved one. I have asked about the significance of this custom of burying familiar objects with the body, and, apparently, at present it is done with no reference to a future life of the spirit, but seems to come from a feeling that the body itself will sleep more peacefully with its treasures about it. Perhaps it is something the same feeling that we have when we do not like to take a wedding-ring off from a dead finger, and try to do with the deserted body whatever the living friend would have liked. It seems to me that it is probably the survival of a custom beyond the belief that prompted it, for so many races bury things with their dead that it is hoped will be of use in the future life, and Shintō is so old and so vague, that this custom may have originated in that way, and then lost one meaning and gained another in the course of ages.

Wednesday, at one o'clock, the funeral took place. I received a card announcing the time, and etiquette required that I should either attend the funeral myself, send something to the house, or send some one in my place. Miné and I each sent flowers to the house, with men to carry them in the procession to the grave. Miné sent two huge bouquets of japonicas and plum blossoms, each as large as a man could carry, and I sent one. Each bouquet was set in a stand of green bamboo, with the name of the donor in large letters on the stand, and carried by a white-robed coolie with a queer, black cap on his head.

Miné went early, and attended the ceremony at the house, but advised me not to, as they might not know what to do with a foreigner, and I might find the ceremony difficult to go through, as all who attend are expected to do a certain amount of bowing, both to the family and to the dead. Accordingly, with some of the other members of our household, I went to the house and left my card, then we waited near by in our kurumas until the procession started. At its head rode one of the servants of the family as marshal, then came a few policemen, next the flower-bearers marching two by two, followed by the great white coffin carried on poles on men's shoulders, then the family and near friends in carriages, and, last of all, a train of kurumas containing teachers, school-friends, and others. The day was dismal and drizzling, the roads were very muddy, and the ride to the cemetery was a long one. When we reached it, we stopped in front of a chapel, before which were drawn up two lines of Shintō priests, dressed in stiff white silk robes and wearing stiff black caps. They were producing wild and dismal sounds from various wind instruments and drums, — sounds that, I should think, must have been originally invented to take the place of the wailing for the dead that we still find practiced among so many barbarous races.

We went first, not into the chapel, but to a little house near by, where we sat for a while, and tea was served before we were summoned to the chapel. There are several such houses about the chapel, and this one had been set apart for the use of the pupils and teachers of the Peeresses' School. Here I had for the first time an opportunity to notice that all of the girls were in Japanese full dress,—a kimono of some plain colored crape, with the mon or crest stamped on the back and sleeves in white. With this costume two white silk undergarments are worn, showing along the edges of the dark kimono. It seems that this dress is the correct thing for funerals as well as for more cheerful social gatherings.

Soon we were summoned to the chapel, where we found the family and near friends already seated. The coffin occupied the back of the room in the centre, and in front of it a Shintō priest in white silk was reading aloud from a scroll. He was kneeling, and I supposed that it was a prayer, but learned afterward that it was an account of our little friend's short life. The school-girls were much moved by it, and the scene was most impressive. After the priest had finished, the wild music began again, a small stand was brought and placed in front of the coffin, and another stand on which were a quantity of green sprays, each tied with a white paper streamer, was placed in front of one of the priests. Then the girl's elder brother, the one of the family nearest to her in age, came forward, clothed in a white mourning garment and with straw shoes on his feet. The priest handed him a green spray, he placed it on the table in front of the coffin, stepped back three paces, and bowed low in a last farewell to his sister. After him came the other brothers and sisters, dressed in white, the girls with their hair flowing and tied just at the neck with a white cord. After them the father and mother, the near friends, and last of all those less intimate, placed each a single spray upon the coffin and bowed farewell. I went among the last, and bowed my good-by to my little pupil just as I had so often bowed to her in school. This was the end of the ceremony, and we went back to the house until the coffin had been carried to the grave, and then came away. The relatives and intimate friends followed the coffin to the grave and saw it lowered. The green sprays were placed upon it and a tall wooden post set over it, to be replaced at the end of a year by a stone. I was curious to know why the elder brother was the chief mourner when the child's parents were living, and made inquiries on that point. I was told that in Japan there is no ceremonial mourning for those below one in rank, consequently parents never wear mourning for a child, nor indeed is it common for the parents to even attend the funeral, although in this instance they broke through the custom and went. There is no reason why the parents should not go to a ball to-morrow, so far as the etiquette of the country is concerned. Hence the person in the family who is nearest of kin and next below in rank to the deceased is the chief mourner. He is the first to bow before the coffin at the funeral, and walks first in the funeral procession, and the prescribed period of mourning is longer for him than for any of the rest of the family.

I asked also about the significance of the green sprays. They are for purification. Death here, as among the Jews, carries defilement, and the particular tree from which the branches were taken is supposed to be purifying in its touch. When the funeral ceremony is over, as a last act all who have attended it and so subjected themselves to the defilement of death purify themselves before going back to the world again; having done this, they bow their farewell and leave the body, and the branches are laid away with it in the grave.

March 29.

The excitements of the past week have been an earthquake and a wedding. The earthquake took place the night before last, and is the third quite lively one that we have had this winter. It is true that one does become more afraid of earthquakes the more one knows of them, and this last one really frightened me a good deal, partly, I think, because it occurred in the dead of night, waking me out of a sound sleep, and so taking me at a disadvantage. People are beginning to feel as if these unusually lively shakes might be premonitions of something worse, although I should suppose that Bandai San might be enough of an explosion to let off steam for some time to come.

I do not know exactly how far Yasaku's matrimonial affairs had gone when I last wrote about them, but I think he was just looking about in a general way for a wife. Since then his father and brother have been down to spend the day with him twice, and to them he confided the delicate task of picking out for him a bride in Utsu-no-miya, and bringing her down to Tōkyō. One day my maid-servant announced to me that Yasaku's wife was coming to him the next day, and we were all in quite a flurry of excitement over the news. Yasaku himself had put down new mats in his room, had purchased a complete set of housekeeping things, and had even gone to the length of pawning his summer clothes for the sake of having some stylish cards with his name on them in Japanese and Roman letters, though of the latter alphabet he is totally ignorant. The next day was terribly rainy, but Yasaku was cheerful and expectant. He expended about two dollars in the purchase of a fine wedding feast, and when evening came and no wife had appeared, Yasaku began to feel rather mad, especially as there would not be another lucky day for the marriage within ten days or a fortnight, and no Japanese of his class would dare to be married on any but a lucky day. When it finally became evident that the bride was not coming, Yasaku wrote a letter to his relatives, in which he said that if they really meant to get him a wife, he wished they would send her along without further delay, and that if she failed to appear on the next lucky day, he would not have her at all, but they could keep her in Utsu-no-miya, and he would hunt up a wife for himself in Tōkyō. This scathing epistle apparently had the desired effect, for last Monday, by the first train, the bride and a number of relatives came to town, and for two days I saw nothing of Yasaku, as he was busy entertaining the wedding party. Tuesday morning, Miné and I each received a tribute from the bride in the shape of a box containing about fifteen nice fresh country eggs, and Tuesday evening, O Kaio, my maid, brought in the bride to pay her respects to me. She was a fat, round-faced country girl, and she came in looking very much dazed and overawed. She had probably never been so near to a foreigner before, and I am quite sure that my foreign parlor was as strange to her as it would be to a South Sea Islander. She plumped down on her knees before me, and put her forehead on the carpet, and there she remained until O Kaio got her up and convoyed her out. She hardly dared look at me at all, and was so visibly embarrassed that I hardly dared look at her for fear she would turn and flee. To-day, I went down to the stable, ostensibly to see the horse, but really to see the bride. On her own ground her manners are pleasant and not too awestricken, and the funny little three-mat room with its miniature housekeeping arrangements looked very clean and cheerful. She will be in clover for a Japanese wife among the lower classes, for she has no mother-in-law to order her around, and Yasaku is an extremely good-tempered fellow, not given to drink, and with a magnificent income of ten yen a month. She will have nothing to do except cook the meals and take care of the clothes, so it is a very good situation for her, though her tenure of office cannot be considered certain.

Sunday, March 31.

I have been devoting most of my day to answering in writing some puzzling questions on John's Gospel, and cannot add much more to this letter to-night. I have asked the members of my Sunday-school class to bring in questions in writing, as they do not trust their English enough to ask many in the class, and then I put the answers in writing too, that they may study them at their leisure. I enjoy it very much, but it takes some time, and I have been three Sundays answering a list of twenty-five questions that one boy brought in, for many of them required quite long and full answers. I think I shall be able to write a commentary on John very soon, at this rate; in fact, I feel as if I had written one already.

Here are a few of the questions: —

"Why did Jesus call himself not the Son of God, but the Son of Man?"

"In John ii. 4, what is the general meaning of Jesus' answer to his mother? This demeanor of our Lord is very dissimilar to his usual meekness and patience. Why he behaved thus in this case, and once in verses 15, 16, St. Mark, chap. xi.?"

"God is love, not anger. Nevertheless it is recorded that 'the wrath of God abideth on him.' Is there no inconsistency?"

These are only a few, but will give you a fair idea of the thoughtful way in which my boys are studying. It has increased my own interest in the class very much to have such questions handed in, but of course the answering of them carefully and clearly has required a great deal of thought and time on my part, and my Sundays have been pretty busy lately in consequence.

CHAPTER XI.

April 6 to 14.

A Country Walk. — Feast of Dolls at a Daimiō's Yashiki. — Picnic at Mito Yashiki. — A Day at the Theatre. — Japanese Acting.

Tōkyō, April 6, 1889.

Our vacation began on Wednesday, and in the morning Miné and I went out to see Yuki at her country house, where she was spending a day or two. She and her husband with servants and children move back and forth between city and country houses in the most surprising and independent manner. The house is entirely finished now, though as yet only partly furnished, and its master takes great delight in it, and spends all his holidays there with his wife and children. He roams about the place, overseeing the workmen who are laying out the grounds, and Yuki takes walks with the children, and enjoys the freedom from the restraint that her social position entails upon her in the city.

When we reached the gate, we found her at the head of a train of children and nurses, just starting for a walk. A very picturesque sight they were, Yuki so bright and pretty in her soft-colored Japanese garments, and the five little ones, in their many-hued, quaint, wide-sleeved robes, dancing back and forth and around her like so many butterflies. They were tumbling over each other and their mother like five unruly puppies, and were enjoying themselves in the most uproarious manner. We found that they were on their way down into the fields to gather a plant that is used here to mix into a kind of cake, so Miné and I joined the company and wandered about, talking with Yuki and watching the children, who were very busy grubbing up all sorts of plants and bringing them to their mother to pronounce judgment upon. Bōt' chan had the services of a policeman (his father's bodyguard), who carried him over the ditches and helped him to find the plants, while the little girls were attended by their nurses, so we had nothing to do but enjoy ourselves, and a very pleasant time we had.

Miné stayed to lunch, but as I was on horseback, I was obliged to go home and change my dress and come out again in my kuruma, for we were going that afternoon to see the feast of dolls at the house of one of the Tokugawa daimiōs. Miné has an aunt who is one of the ladies-in-waiting in the house, and through her Miné secured permission to bring me to see the ancestral dolls when the feast came around to that house.

Most of Japan celebrated the feast a month ago, but at this Tokugawa Yashiki they are so conservative that they do not keep the national feasts by the new calendar, but begin their year just when the rest of Japan would be beginning it now, if Commodore Perry had never put them into communication with the outside world; and their feasts come trailing along a month or two after the same celebration in more modernized houses. In this house, more than in almost any other in Tōkyō, one finds the old-time etiquette kept up, and so little have the recent changes affected the lives of the dwellers within this quiet place, that many of the ladies in the house had probably never seen a foreigner in their lives until the day when I called upon them. Miné gave me a little instruction in the art of getting down on my knees and putting my forehead on the floor, but the present style of American dress makes it very hard to do the thing gracefully, and my joints are a good deal too stiff to allow me to be comfortable during the process. However, I did it after a fashion, and felt very much like a fool in doing it, but it seemed necessary for me to show my appreciation of the kindness that had been shown me by being polite in some manner that my entertainers could recognize. Our good manners are so undemonstrative that only a very much foreignized Japanese can discover that we have any at all, and the usual result of an effort here in Japan to copy foreign manners is a complete disregard of all rules of politeness, whether Japanese or foreign.

Well, to go back to our feast of dolls, — after much groveling and doubling up to the many waiting-women who came to the door to receive us, we were ushered into the room where the dolls were set out. There were five or six red-covered shelves, arranged like a flight of steps, running the whole length of the long room, — about twenty feet, I should think, — and these were completely filled with the dolls and their belongings, some of them hundreds of years old. The dolls were, for the most part, effigies of the Emperor and Empress, and the five court musicians, though there were some of lower rank, but they were not as interesting to me as the delightful little dishes and utensils illustrating perfectly all the furnishings of Japanese homes. Many of the things were of solid silver, most delicately wrought; others were of beautiful lacquer, with the Tokugawa crest upon them. There was a lacquered norimono, such as great people always used until the overthrow of the shogunate and the introduction of the foreign style of coach, and a lacquered bullock-cart, the Emperor's private conveyance in early times. Such a collection of toys would be a delightful thing to take to America, for it is historical, and has been making for hundreds of years, and illustrates ancient as well as recent Japanese life.

Before each Emperor and Empress was

set a fine Japanese dinner on tiny lacquered trays, with cups, bowls, chopsticks, and plates, all complete, and each dish containing its proper food. There was the little saké pot, filled with the sweet, white saké that is brewed especially for this feast; there was the big rice bowl with its spoon beside it, and everything ready for their majesties to step down and eat. The food is renewed three times a day for three days, and then the feast of dolls is over, and the dolls and their belongings are carefully packed and put away in the fireproof storehouses where all valuables are kept.

When we had finished looking at the dolls, and had partaken first of coffee and then of tea, because we were afraid that it would not be polite to refuse either beverage, word was sent that the master and mistress of the house would like to see us. We were conducted to a waiting-room, where fortunately there were chairs, so I felt more at home than I had when sitting on the floor, and there we waited for some time. By Miné's advice I had brought with me a present for the master of the house, of American photographs, some of them views of the city of Washington, and others of Colorado scenery, and these we had sent in upon our arrival. While we were waiting for my lord and my lady to appear, domestics served us with tea and sushi or rice sandwiches, and the year-old baby was brought in and exhibited. At last there was a rustle of silken garments in the long corridor, and the daimiō, a young man of about twenty, in Japanese costume, appeared, with his wife, an extremely pretty little girl, not quite sixteen years old, who looked altogether too much like a child to be the mother of the bouncing, red-cheeked baby that we had just seen. She is, by the way, the younger daughter of the last of the Shoguns. The young man spoke a little English, and made an effort at conversation. I do not try my Japanese yet with great people, as I am afraid that I shall not be polite enough, though I can get along pretty well now with servants and shop-keepers.

At last the daimiō wished to know whether I had brought my dog, and when I said that he was without the honorable gate, or rather when Miné had said it for me, the party adjourned to the porch to watch him while I threw sticks for him and made him beg for sponge cake. The little wife was so pleased that she seized the astonished Bruce about the neck and embraced him, entirely regardless of her elegant crape dress, and then we went off, Bruce trotting behind my kuruma, fairly covered with glory. Miné's aunt had been much pleased with Bruce when she saw him go through his tricks in my parlor, and I think I owe my invitation to visit at that house to her glowing accounts of my wonderful dog.

I was given, in return for my photographs, a baby doll creeping on all fours, dressed in crape; a black and white puppy with raw-silk hair; a silk-covered box; and a chopstick case of silk. The doll is an uncommonly nice one, of Kyōtō workmanship, and quite old. All the sushi that I had been unable to eat were sent out to my kuruma, neatly done up in white paper.

April 14.

Yuki had been planning a picnic nearly every day since our vacation began, but whenever we had our arrangements all made to go on a certain day it would rain, and force us to give it up. Monday was my reception day, and I ought to have stayed at home, but as it was pleasant at last, we went on the long-postponed picnic, and had a charming day in the gardens of Mito Yashiki. These gardens are the most beautiful in Tōkyō, unless the Emperor's own are better. They were made in the feudal times by the Prince of Mito, and the place is still called the Mito Yashiki, though the old daimiō mansion is pulled down, and on its site stands a great arsenal. The pile of brick buildings and tall factory chimneys makes the street front of this yashiki one of the most modernized spots in all Tōkyō, and though I have passed the place a great many times, I never suspected that behind all that brick and mortar was hidden one of the loveliest bits of Old Japan that remains in the city. It requires a special permit from the Minister of War to secure admission to the garden, and only the favored few ever see its beauties.

The garden is laid out in the Japanese landscape style, which is so like nature that it is difficult to believe that the wooded hills, the lakes, and lawns, and running streams, have been put in place by human hands. The garden is two hundred years old, I am told, and the trees have grown so large that the woods might be primeval forest. Here and there, peeping out from among the green shadows, are small temples, modeled after celebrated shrines in China and Japan. By the little lake, and almost overhanging it, there is a lovely summer-house, built by the daimiō for his own use, but now modified for the pleasure parties that are invited here. There is a dancing-room with a waxed hard-wood floor, and a dining-room fitted up in foreign style with table and chairs, and with glass instead of paper in the shōji or sliding screens. We spent most of our time on the veranda and on the smooth green lawn in front of the summer-house, where the children were playing and picking flowers all day long. One beautiful flowering cherry-tree trailed its drooping branches almost to the grass, and the whole scene — the children in their bright-colored flowing robes, their hands full of flowers, the men-servants and maid-servants following them about, the green lawn, the blue water, the background of hills and woods with here and there a red-lacquered, heavy-roofed temple peeping out — made a picture of all that is most attractive in this Japanese life. It was perfect in its way. We had a charming day, and were more than ever glad that we went when we did, as we awoke the next morning to find the rain coming down in torrents.

Wednesday we went to the theatre, a party of five, — two foreign and three Japanese ladies, — just the number to fill a box. The play was a part of the story of the forty-seven rōnins, and was given at the best theatre and by the best actors in Tōkyō. It is the most popular of all Japanese plays, and we had a great deal of trouble in securing a box, for there are such crowds going every day that boxes have to be engaged a long time beforehand. I am told that whenever a theatrical manager finds his audiences growing thin he produces this play, and the people at once flock to see it.

Instead of buying tickets at the theatre itself, in this part of the world you have to buy them at a tea-house; then when you go, you visit the tea-house first, and there leave your extra wraps and anything else that you do not care to take to the theatre. Here, too, you partake of a cup of tea, and are then escorted to the theatre and ushered to your seat by one of the employees of the tea-house. Then all day long the tea-house men look after you, — bring you tea, oranges, cake, and lunches of all descriptions, escort you back to your room in the tea-house between the acts, and care for you in every possible or imaginable way. We left home at about ten in the morning, and reached home again at eight in the evening; so you see that theatre-going here is quite an undertaking, and one not to be entered upon lightly nor in term time.

I shall not undertake to tell you much about the play, for you can read the story in Mitford's "Tales of Old Japan," or in Greey's "Loyal Rōnins." I am not a dramatic critic, and my judgment of the acting is not worth much, but I will try to give you something of the impression that the whole thing made upon me.

In the first place, the scenery and costumes were good, and carefully studied historically, and carried the audience at once out of the end of the nineteenth century and back to the Japan of the Tokugawas. The acting, so far as gestures and movements of the face and body went, seemed to me almost perfect. The voices were, to my ear, strained and unnatural, but I cannot judge very well about that, as I am not yet sufficiently familiar with the Japanese voice under stress of violent emotion, to know how it ought to sound. The fact that all the female parts are taken by men is a disadvantage so far as illusion is concerned, for dress and act as they may, the hoarse croak which is the conventional voice for women on the Japanese stage is a drawback to one's enjoyment of the feminine acting.

At one side of the stage, hidden by a screen, was a chorus with instruments of music, who gave in a sort of chant the thoughts of the principal performers at times when our stage customs would introduce a soliloquy, and the actor was thus left with nothing to do but to look and act his part. This chorus also introduced occasional comments on the events of the play, thus keeping the sympathies of the audience flowing in the right direction, and making it quite plain who was to be pitied and who blamed.

The play itself was a little too gory to suit our present taste, as there were two suicides and three murders performed upon the stage, with every ghastly detail of blood, muscular contortion, death-rattle, and final rigidity given in the most carefully worked out and realistic manner. The play was, however, immensely interesting in spite of the gore. I think that that day spent at the theatre has given me a great deal better insight into the moral perspective of the Japanese mind than anything else could have done. As I watched the progress of the play, I began to understand more fully than I had before that passion of loyalty that made revenge the one object in life of those forty-seven men, and which made it altogether right and just that they should sell their wives into the worst of slaveries, sever all their domestic relations, kill their own nearest relatives, and give themselves up to any or every crime or vice, if by so doing they could further the object that was foremost in their thoughts and first among their duties. That the acting was good I am quite sure, or I could not have spent eight mortal hours on an uncomfortable seat, in a house foul with tobacco smoke and all manner of evil smells, watching a play, the spirit of which was so utterly foreign to my own ideas of right and wrong, and been so entirely carried away by the thing that I forgot all the discomforts and was for the time wholly in sympathy both with the ends sought and the means used by the conspirators.

CHAPTER XII.

April 19 to May 2.

The Empress' Visit. — Presentation to the Empress. — A Buddhist Funeral. — A Garden Party. — Questions on John's Gospel.

Tōkyō, April 19, 1889.

I must write up the Empress' visit while it is fresh in my mind, so as to give you as complete a picture as possible of it, and then hereafter, when I write "the Empress came to see us yesterday," you will know exactly what that means. Mrs. Shimoda sent me word on Tuesday that the Empress was coming on Thursday and would visit my class, so I had time to find out from Miné exactly what I was to do and what I was not to do, and to work myself up into a fine state of excitement for fear my bows would not be deep enough or long enough to show proper honor to an imperial visitor.

When we reached the school on Thursday morning, we found that her Majesty's baggage had already arrived, and as we came up the staircase we caught glimpses of beautiful lacquered things and gorgeous silver smoking-sets, that were standing at the head of the stairs waiting to be carried into the Empress' private apartments. There was a look of preparation about the place, and all the school attendants were rushing around in great excitement, apparently doing nothing but talking, but perhaps really accomplishing something. When we went to the teachers' room and looked out into the yard, we found it full of blue-clad coolies, who were resting in all stages of *déshabille* by the litters and trucks on which they had brought the "honorable baggage." The teachers were arrayed in their best clothes, and while the ladies appeared quite calm, the gentlemen were rushing about distractedly, with hair on end and collars and neckties all awry.

Mrs. Shimoda was fairly in her element, for she is thoroughly at home in court ceremonies of all kinds, and knows exactly the right thing to do upon such occasions as this. In the general excitement, the bell-ringer forgot to ring the bell at the right time, and school began nearly half an hour late.

I learned after my arrival that I was to have only one class during the morning, as the members of my two higher classes had been set to work in the cooking department to show their skill by preparing a dinner for the distinguished guests. This change from our regular programme left me with nothing to think of but my lesson before the Empress; and my dread of it, and especially of the ordeal of greeting her properly, grew with the thinking. I practiced up my bows with Miné the last thing before she went to her class, and then sat me down to wait with my heart in my boots until the dreaded moment should arrive. However, I was not without distractions, for as I was sitting by the window, I became suddenly aware of four fine carriages occupying the girls' tennis ground, and began to think that the Empress must have arrived without my knowing it. I concluded, however, at last that she would hardly have come in a plain black carriage, as from my experience of their habits I had gained the idea that the imperial family always went about in red and gold coaches. That my conclusions were correct was proved very soon afterward by the arrival of a gorgeous mounted official, who rode up to the front door where a guard was stationed, said something to him, and rode off again. Soon the hall was lined with a double row of ladies, for the first four carriages had brought the Empress' attendants, and they were now in readiness to receive her. The next arrival was a mounted soldier carrying a small purple silk flag with a gold chrysanthemum embroidered on it. This was taken into the house. Then came quite a cavalcade of soldiers carrying red and white pennons, and last of all the red and gold coach that I had been expecting. A gentleman stepped forward with a mat and laid it on the doorstep, the ladies came out to the carriage, bowed very low, and then formed a double line to the door. Then the Empress alighted and walked in between the ladies, followed by her two companions who had come in the carriage with her.

That was the last I saw of her for a while, and I had to content myself with watching the grooms, who were at work on the playground taking out the horses and washing the red and gold coach. At last the clapper sounded, I seized my book, braced myself up, and went down to my class. The girls were in a state of great excitement, and at first I found it very hard to command their attention. There was a beautiful lacquered chair standing close by my desk, — black lacquer, with gold chrysanthemums and a purple brocade seat. We had just begun the lesson when there was a rush along the hall and the recitation-room door was flung wide open. The girls rose in their places, and I turned toward the door, expecting to see the Empress standing there, but no one appeared but a tousle-headed little secretary, who gazed distractedly into the room, muttered incoherently, and then shut the door with a bang. The girls dropped back into their seats, my heart began to beat again, and we went on with the lesson. All was going well again when once more there was a sound of hurrying feet, once more the door was flung noisily open, and once more the tousle-headed secretary looked wildly in, talking vociferously the while to another man whom he had in tow. Then he slammed the door and rushed off again, and my pupils and I had a good laugh to work off our nervousness, for these preliminary scares had not done much toward calming us.

At last there was a rustle of silken skirts in the hall, and we knew that our hour was come. The door opened, and Mrs. Shimoda looked in. The girls rose, and we all stood with down-dropped heads until her Majesty appeared. Then we bowed very low and very slowly, kept our heads down until I thought I should suffocate, and then lifted them slowly up again. By this time the Empress was seated in the lacquered chair, the girls could take their seats again, and we could go on with the lesson.

When I went into the class and saw the excitement of the pupils, I thought that if they were so nervous beforehand they would make no kind of show when the Empress should finally appear; but there is where I did not fully understand my little peeresses. From the moment there was need for it they showed the most perfect self-possession, and I have never had better or less timid recitations in my life than those that they made in the Empress' presence. Our visitor stayed for nearly half an hour, listening most interestedly, although she could not understand a word that was said, and by the time she left the room I had caught several good glimpses of her, although, of course, I had no time for staring, even if that had been the proper thing for me to do. These glimpses revealed a small, slender woman (though that, of course, need hardly be said), rather loaded down by her heavy dove-colored silk dress and dove-colored Paris bonnet with a white plume. Her face seemed to me a sad one, with a patient look about it that was pathetic. They say that she is a very intellectual woman, and one of great strength and beauty of character.

After every girl in the class had made a recitation, Mrs. Shimoda went up to the Empress and bowed, then our guest rose, the class rose, and we all bowed, remaining with our heads within about three feet of the floor until her Majesty was well out of the room. Then the ordeal was over, or at least I thought it was, and I went on with the recitation feeling quite light hearted.

At last the clapper sounded, and I dismissed the class, and was very glad to go upstairs to my desk and talk the whole thing over with Miné, who, it seems, had been sent for to explain in case the Empress should ask any questions, and had been standing just outside of my door all through the recitation hour. When I looked out of the window, I found that the grooms had finished washing the red and gold carriage, and had covered it entirely over with a green damask silk cover, decorated with an enormous gold-embroidered chrysanthemum. I had nothing at all to do for the next hour but to read and congratulate myself on being through with the Empress for the day, but when that period was over and Miné came back from her class, the same breathless and wild-haired little secretary who had bothered me downstairs came in, and announced that the Empress would receive the foreign teachers as well as the head Japanese teachers. Miné had barely time to tell us what to do, as they were waiting for us then, and we were obliged to hurry off very little prepared for this new interview with royalty. Miné told us to follow her to the door of the room so as to see exactly what she did, though we must not go in until our turn came, and then one at a time. As I was following this suggestion and moving toward a position in front of the door, I was seized and held by my old enemy, the little secretary, who had evidently taken the idea into his erratic little head that unless physical force were applied to restrain her, that outside barbarian would rush right into the imperial presence; consequently I did not reach the door at all to see how Miné did the thing. She came back, however, very soon, bearing a large white paper bundle, and had just time to tell me what to do when I should receive a similar one before Mrs. Shimoda beckoned to me, and it was my turn to go in. This is the order of ceremonies through which I had to go in paying my respects to the Empress. Upon the threshold of the door I bowed once, then walked straight ahead until I was directly in front of the Empress, who was sitting at the other end of the room, at right angles to the door. Here I turned to my right so as to face her, stepped a step forward, and bowed. Then a gentleman came up to me with a tray on which was a large white paper bundle. This I took, lifted up to my breast, put my head down to it, bowed again, and backed out, bowing once more at the door. In handling the bundle, I had to take pains to hold it high, as it is disrespectful to the giver to hold a present any way but directly in front of you and as high as possible.

The bundles contained pieces of beautiful white silk (twenty-five yards or thereabouts in each piece), worth here about twenty dollars or so, and at home possibly twice as much, not reckoning any fancy value that may attach to anything given by the Empress of Japan. In old times, such a gift as that, carried into the country districts, would have been worshiped as holy, and I noticed that when I showed it to Yasaku he took off his cap to it, and stood in a most reverential attitude as he looked at it. A few years ago, a garment made of silk received from such a source would have been thought to possess miraculous qualities.

The Empress spent the whole day at the school, coming at nine and staying until school was dismissed at three. At last, when her Imperial Majesty had been escorted to her carriage and had driven off with her horsemen and her footmen, her banners, and her lords-in-waiting and ladies-in-waiting, we picked up our books, skipped into our kurumas, and rattled off home, rather tired by such a long strain of excitement and grandeur. I was very glad, too, when I reached home, to order my horse and have a good ride to limber me up and make me feel myself once more a free American woman after all my unaccustomed bowing and cringing.

May 2.

I have just been to a Buddhist funeral, that of the mother of one of my friends. The ceremonies are much more complicated than those of the Shintō, though they were not, to my mind, so impressive. I did not go to the house, as I had been the day before and left my card, and I was afraid that I might be in the way there, but went straight to the cemetery, and there with an American friend and a great many Japanese awaited the arrival of the funeral procession.

The day was terribly rainy, and the mud was very deep, so that we had quite a dirty walk from the house where we waited to the little chapel where the funeral ceremonies were conducted. The chapel is the same one in which Shintō services were held at the funeral that I have already written you about. At this Buddhist ceremony, the coffin was placed at the entrance instead of being at the back of the room. The building was nearly filled with people when we entered, but an usher, when he learned our names, led us at once to seats reserved for us.

The ceremony was a long one, performed by a number of gorgeously attired priests. There were candles burning before the coffin, incense was burned, prayers were intoned, rosaries were rattled, and there was a great deal of chanting by a chorus of priests, as well as beating of drums and blowing of wind instruments. A bell was rung at intervals during the services, and the effect of the whole ritual was Roman Catholic. The priests themselves one could have picked out as ecclesiastics anywhere, by their faces. The ceremony ended as the Shintō ceremony does, with an opportunity for every one to go up and make a bow before the coffin, only in this case each person placed a grain of incense on the incense burner before making the farewell bow, instead of laying a green spray before the coffin as in the Shintō ceremony. I hoped that I might not have to do that, as I did not know its significance, and was not sure whether it was bowing down to strange gods or not; but when I found that I could not get out of it without being rude and possibly seeming to dishonor the dead, I thought of what Elisha said to Naaman about bowing down in the temple of Rimmon, and concluded that this was a similar case; so when my turn came I went up, offered my incense, and made my bow with a clear conscience.

Saturday afternoon, there was a garden party at Count Okuma's country place, to which I went under the escort of American friends. The garden is a lovely one. There was a band hidden in one part of the grounds, refreshment booths were everywhere, day fireworks constantly going up, and a great many agreeable people wandering about. We walked around in a desultory fashion, stopping to talk whenever we met an acquaintance, and spent a very pleasant afternoon.

My Sunday-school scholars continue to send me in written questions, many of them quite curious and rather puzzling. I shall have written a complete compendium of theology pretty soon, if they keep on. Here are some recent ones: —

"I have learned only a little about the devil, that is, the king of evils; it was an angel, but by committing the sin of spirit fell to the devil. A well-known Japanese Buddhist says that he has investigated for many years whence the devil came, but he never found it. And this is the chief point in which Japanese Buddhists argue against Christianity and many of my best friends offend. Teach me about the devil as much as is in the Bible, and also the references if you please."

"M. Renan and the followers of critical school says Jesus was born in Nazareth not Bethlehem as the sacred writers affirms, but on the other hand the Evangelists had ascribed his birthplace to the small town of Bethlehem to make ancient prophets may be fulfilled. In short, the Evangelists deceive us in this matter, and if we read John vii. verses 42, 52, we are confirmed that the rulers of Jews and people was ignorant of Jesus birthplace which is Bethlehem. They hold fast that Jesus was born in Nazareth not Bethlehem. Why? Are the people of Judea all ignorant of his exact birthplace? That is rather improbable, at least it seems to me so. If it was so, at least his parents know it. Then why had not explained the fact to the populace to clear the Christship of Jesus? What was the case of the time?"

CHAPTER XIII.

May 8 to June 22.

Summer Weather. — A Matsuri. — Early School. — Perry Expedition Reports. — Bible Class of School-Girls. — Fighting Fleas. — Japanese Servants. — The New School-Building. — The Peeresses' Literary Society. — A Speech by Mr. Knapp. — Scandal.

Tōkyō, May 8, 1889.

The summer is coming on, indeed is in full blast so far as flowers are concerned, but we still have many damp, cloudy days and many cold, windy ones, and the air does not feel very summery yet. It may warm up to the white-dress season any day, but to-day I am inclined to shiver, as I sit writing in my winter clothes with no fire. The azaleas are in full bloom now and are lovely. The large ones of all colors that we cultivate so carefully in hot-houses at home are entirely hardy here, and bloom in the greatest profusion. The wistaria is in blossom too, and all Tōkyō is sweet with the fragrance of these two flowers. The maple-trees have hung out their delicate red leaves, much redder than in their autumn brilliance. They are of an infinite variety of shapes and colors, some delicate as fern leaves, others a perfect star shape, and in every shade from pink, through brilliant scarlet, to deepest copper and maroon.

Last night a party of us went out for a pleasure stroll, chaperoned by Mrs. Watanabe, Miné's sweet-faced little cousin, and escorted by my faithful Cook San, bearing a lantern. There was a great matsuri or festival in progress not far from our house, and we walked over there to mingle with the holiday crowd and see the sights. Of course we could not have done such a thing in any great American city on account of the drunken men and the rowdies, but here there are no disorderly persons upon such occasions, so that a trip of this kind is perfectly safe, though not altogether conventional. On both sides of the street that runs by the temple where the festival is held were little booths, their fronts lighted by flaring kerosene torches. Some of the booths contained trifles for sale, flowers, candy, cakes, hairpins, wooden ware, goldfish, baskets, — anything and everything that the festival-goers might like to take home as gifts to their stay-at-home friends. At one place two men were engaged in the manufacture of candy, pulling it as we do molasses candy, and working it into all manner of shapes with great skill. We stopped and watched them for a long time, buying six cents' worth of candy as a sort of fee for the entertainment. Other booths had curtains hung in front of them and wonderful pictures of the shows to be seen within. Outside of one or two stood a man, crying, or rather chanting, the various excellences of his show, and whetting the curiosity of the audience that he gathered out of the crowd by lifting the curtain for a second and then letting it fall again.

We went into two of the shows, paying the admission fee of one sen for the sake of seeing what lay behind the mystic curtain. The first was a theatrical performance by monkeys, which to me seemed really quite wonderful. The monkeys were finely dressed in old-style Japanese costume, and they acted very well, — fighting, weeping, rolling their eyes, trembling, and displaying all sorts of human emotions by gestures and facial expression. It is a mystery to me how they can be taught to do such things just at the proper moment without any appreciation of the part they are performing, but they did it in the most surprisingly natural manner.

Our second entrance fee took us into a juggler's booth, where an emaciated young man in foreign dress was doing some exceedingly transparent sleight-of-hand tricks, and it was so stupid that we were afraid we were not going to get our money's worth of amusement. However, when the young man had finished, a girl came out in a long, embroidered kimono, and in that cumbersome but graceful dress performed very cleverly upon the slack rope, so we felt that our admission fee had not been wasted after all. These were the only shows that we entered, as the others seemed to be monstrosities or horrors of one sort or another that we did not care to see. The signs outside pictured men shaped like crabs, women with necks so long that they could sit still while their heads wandered all over the house, ghosts, bogies, a series of puppets representing the life and death of Nishino, the murderer of Mr. Mori, and various other penny-dreadful attractions.

On our way home we stopped at a flower show, and bought a thriving rosebush in full bloom for six sen, and two large, blooming pinks in pots for one sen each. While we were making our purchases, the mother of one of our little pupils met us, and insisted that we must come into her house near by and rest before going home. She was so urgent that although it was after nine o'clock, an unprecedentedly late hour for visiting in Tōkyō, we could not refuse, but went in and stayed for about half an hour, drinking tea, eating cake, and conversing in Japanese. The house was a charming one, in the daintiest Japanese style, and the host and hostess courteous and delightful.

After this week our school is to begin at half past seven, instead of at half past eight as it has done all winter. I do not enjoy rising at six as I must hereafter, but it will nevertheless be a convenient arrangement for me for one reason, — my day's work will be over by half past ten, leaving me still a long day ahead for anything I may wish to do with it.

May 25.

I have been very much interested lately in reading the official reports of the Perry expedition to Japan. The books were given me before I left America, but I did not find them as interesting as I do now that I know the country and the people from actual study of them on their own ground. One part of the interest to me lies in the fact that many of the names mentioned in the Perry reports as names of high officials with whom the American ambassadors had to do are the names of the fathers and grandfathers of my pupils.

I am trying now to start a little Bible class among our school-girls, which will meet at my house on Sunday afternoons, simply to read and talk over the Bible in English. There seems at present a pretty good opening for it, as my class at Mr. Kozaki's meets in the morning, and I shall have plenty of time for the other in the afternoon. I invited two of the girls to come last Sunday, and find that they can understand the simple English of Matthew and Luke quite easily, although of course there are a good many words that are new to them. These girls of ours are very sweet and pure and kind, but they seem to me to have very little that is high or ennobling to occupy their thoughts or to strive after in their lives, and I am sure that the opening of Christian truth to their minds will be a great help to them, filling a place that is now entirely empty, or perhaps I might better say, expanding the soul in a direction where it is now shut in and cramped. I do hope that I can interest them in the study of the Bible so that they will go on and learn more, for there are opportunities enough in Tōkyō now for the study, if I can only get them up to the point where they care about it.

June 2.

Our warm weather has come at last. It began with the month, and to-day I am wearing my thinnest white dress, and feeling hot in that. One of the evils of a Japanese summer has already begun, in the shape of an army of fleas, whose ancestors have been living for generations in the thick Japanese mats that cover my bedroom floor. To-day I have concluded that either I or the fleas must move, so my three servants are at work in the room overhead, as I write, trying to make things disagreeable for the enemy. They have carried all the mats out of doors, and are now engaged in a vigorous sweeping of the room with insect powder. Occasionally I hear a shout from Yasaku as the enemy make a particularly bold stand for their homes, or a stampede on the part of O Kaio as she retreats before the hopping legions. As for myself, after showing my servants how to use the powder, I fled for fear I should be fatally wounded, but not without carrying a number of the enemy away with me. Bruce is also wrestling with several that even a profuse powdering and brushing could not dislodge from his long hair.

I made some visits yesterday in Tsukiji, and among others called upon a recent arrival in Japan, who is now going through her first amusing and often trying experiences with Japanese servants. She is, I should imagine, a notable housewife, who has been accustomed to making her Chinamen in San Francisco carry out her orders after the strictest fashion, but unless her servants are very different from the ordinary Japanese, she will be doomed to disappointment if she tries to make them do exactly what she tells them, in the way she tells them. The Japanese servant generally does, not what you tell him to, but what he thinks is for your highest good, a characteristic that is quite exasperating at first; but when you have found out by repeated experiments that your servants are usually right and you are usually wrong, you come to submit most meekly to their arrangements, though not without occasional yearnings to be once more in a country where you are competent to conduct your own affairs.

There is an element of uncertainty about all things here below, but that uncertainty seems greater in Japan than elsewhere. I am more and more convinced of the advantages of democracy, as I see the workings of an aristocratic form of government. I do not think I have written you that a beautiful new brick building has been in process of construction for some time past, to be occupied, as soon as finished, by our school. It is quite near here, and Miné and I have watched its growth all winter with great interest, as we thought how pleasant and comfortable the new building would seem after the ramshackle old one that we now occupy. It is all finished now, and workmen are engaged in laying out the grounds, and in taking up the trees and shrubs from our present school-yard to plant them in the new place; for here in Japan, when you move, you carry with you not only your furniture, but your garden as well, shade trees, turf, and all. For months the school authorities have been busy choosing carpets, curtains, and furniture, and the plan was, after the examinations were over, for us to move into the new building for our graduating exercises. We were to have a fine time, and the Empress was to make us a speech in person. Such were our hopes and expectations, but at present they seem likely to suffer an untimely blight.

There is another school beside our own under the management of the Imperial Household. It is a school for boys, corresponding in rank with that of our girls, and is called the Peers' School. Last fall it was moved into the buildings of the old Engineering College, and because they were so fine and large a new building was planned for us, that we might be equally well housed. Now, just as our new school-house is finished, the authorities of the boys' school discover that their accommodations are too large, and send in a petition to the Imperial Household Department requesting to be removed to our new building. Of course when I heard of it I simply smiled at the audacity of such a demand, and inquired why they should trouble themselves to make so useless and ridiculous a request, but I am assured that this is no laughing matter, and that there is quite a strong probability that the request will be granted, especially as it is a question of girls' rights against boys' wishes. I am fairly boiling over with wrath, but the worst of it is that there is nothing to do but boil, for our school authorities are as utterly powerless to do anything in the matter as they would be to avert a typhoon or an earthquake that threatened to destroy the building. They cannot even say anything, or write up their wrongs for the newspapers and get public sympathy on their side; they must just smile and submit, and thank the Peers for leaving them the old building instead of trying to grab that too. I am quite curious to see how it will be decided, for I cannot believe that the government will do such a mean thing as take away the building from us.

June 13.

The excitement over the new building increases daily. The teachers talk of resigning in a body, should the building be handed over to the boys, and all who have influence of any kind in any high quarter are using it to turn the scale if possible in our direction.

On Saturday afternoon, the girls had the monthly meeting of their literary society, and as it was their last meeting for the year, and there were to be a number of English recitations and readings, I was urgently requested to be present. This society is quite a different thing from the English society that I have mentioned as meeting at my house, and its monthly programme includes literary exercises of all kinds in Japanese, Chinese, and English. I think that it counts in its membership most of the girls in the school, except the very smallest. The girls run it entirely by themselves, and do very well, if I can judge from my one experience of it. But it was not the society in general, but one occurrence at this meeting, that I wanted to tell you about. As the exercises went on, I noticed that one of our higher-class girls, an extremely interesting girl and a favorite pupil of mine, was looking rather flushed and excited. At last, when her turn came, she rose and began to read something that I supposed to be a poem, from its rhythmic form. As she read, the faces of her listeners grew more and more serious, the reader's voice began to break and quaver, and one by one the heads of the audience drooped, and handkerchiefs were applied to the eyes. Two or three times the reader had to stop altogether, but each time she controlled herself and went on. When she finished and took her seat, every girl and every Japanese teacher in the room was weeping, not quietly and decorously, but passionately, as if under the first sting of some great sorrow, while the reader herself was sobbing as if her heart would break.

Of course, as I could not understand the poem, I was very anxious to know what this tragic thing was that had caused such grief, but when Miné told me, I was not altogether surprised.

It seems that early in the winter this girl had lost a very dear grandmother, who had been to her all her life not only grandmother, but mother and friend as well. I imagine that in a somewhat unhappy home she was the one person whom the poor girl really loved and who really loved her. Since her grandmother's death, the child had been much worried by the thought that she had often been cross and undutiful, and had not repaid the care and love that her grandmother had lavished upon her. This thought had troubled her so that she resolved to do penance by confessing all her shortcomings to her assembled schoolmates, and exhorting them to avoid her errors, and to be always kind and gentle to their dear ones, as the time might soon come when they could never make amends for a hasty word or an undutiful act.

This she did, first writing out her confession in the classical Chinese style, and having it corrected by the Chinese teacher, and then reading it to the girls, with the effect described. It seems to me a most uncommon display of force and courage for a girl of fifteen.

I inclose a clipping from a recent speech of Mr. Knapp, the Unitarian missionary out here, in which he states his mission to Japan more clearly than I have ever known him to state it before. So far as I can make out from his speech, he is here to help the Japanese make a new religion rather than to preach anything as old-fashioned as Christianity. You can, however, judge for yourselves. Here are his own words : —

Sent as I am to your country, not as a missionary but as an ambassador of religion, to see whether the liberal religious sentiment of America can be of any help to you in solving the religious problem of your future, I have no sympathy with those who are seeking to engraft bodily upon your national life a foreign religion. There are, to be sure, many features in that religion which are true and good, and which may be of great help to you. There are none of the great religions of the world which do not contain a great deal of truth; they could not have lived so long and so vitally unless they had been founded upon truth. Of course, then, with your well-known and generous hospitality, you are ever ready to receive from foreign sources whatever commends itself to you as true and good in the world of religious thought. But as Japanese you also have a religious past, and it is upon that, whatever help you may receive from foreign sources, — it is upon that that you will build the fabric of your future religion. And it is not a religious past of which you need be ashamed, if we are to judge of it by its fruits. You have in it many elements of solidity upon which you may build. In the refined sense of honor which characterizes your samurai class, in the thoughtfulness and kindliness which you show to each other, in your care for the rights of the poor, and above all in your sentiment and practice of filial reverence, all of which characteristics are rooted in your past, you furnish a type of morality in many respects far superior to that of the Western world, and if you build your future religion upon that, it will be a religion of which you need never be ashamed. And if in building up such a religion, the liberal religious sentiment of America can aid you, you can rely upon its earnest and brotherly help. For this is the message which I am commissioned to bring to you, — the message not of conversion but of affiliation.

I wonder how much of a church the apostles would have founded if, instead of preaching against the prejudices and preferences of their audiences, they had gone about saying, "We don't want you to change your religion, to give up your old customs, to follow Christ, but we would like you to listen to what we have to say, and then choose from your stock of ideas those that are best suited to your national prejudices. Anything you don't like, you can leave."

I am afraid the Greeks would have been even less moved than they were, if Paul had preached to them that way on Mars' Hill; and even those who might have followed him and added some ideas from his stock to their already heterogeneous assortment would have gained nothing but a new philosophy, with high moral ideas, doubtless, but with no inspiration or power over the life. All Japan to-day is picking and choosing, seeing and hearing, some new thing; and a thing is interesting because it is new; and when it is a year or two old is thrown aside for something newer, and therefore more interesting. What is wanted is not men's assent to new ideas, — there is plenty of that already, — but a working of those ideas into the heart and life of the people, and an upbuilding of character thereby.

June 22.

You probably know that Tōkyō is a terrible place for malicious scandal. One of the regular ways here of attacking any person or any object that is disliked by any one for any reason is by means of scandalous stories, made up on a foundation of truth, or cunningly fitted in with some well-known facts that will give it an air of truth to people who accept and circulate evil reports without investigation. An example of this nasty practice has just come up in the shape of an attack on one of the finest girls' schools in the city, — an attack that has been so successful that they say that there is not a single application for admission to the school this summer where there were hundreds last year at this time. The school is the Koto Jo Gakko, where the Misses Prince teach, with whom I stayed when I first came to Tōkyō. The attack began in a low paper that makes its living by publishing lies of just the kind that were told about the school and its teachers. The stories once started, other low papers took them up, and added to them until they became big enough, and began to look enough like truth, for the more respectable papers to comment on them. Soon the scandal was in the mouths of all Tōkyō. When the school gates were opened in the morning, scurrilous placards were found posted upon them, and as the girls went to school they were insulted by school-boys and students on the street, and all this because of stories which had no foundation, except that one of the teachers had once delivered before the girls a rather foolish and ill-advised lecture on the choice of husbands, in which he had viewed marriage from the somewhat sentimental standpoint of Europe and America, instead of taking the purely business view of it common in Japan. The teacher has been turned off, and possibly the president of the school may be also, as a sacrifice to the public feeling that has been aroused about the matter, and to save the school itself from complete collapse. That this was intended for an attack not simply on the one school, but on female education in general, seems likely from the fact that these same low papers are now busying themselves with some of the more important of the missionary schools for girls, though as yet they have done them no harm. Our turn may come next, but our school is run on such conservative principles that there is less danger.

CHAPTER XIV.

June 29 to July 24.

School-Building Trouble settled. — A Japanese Baby. — Shopping. — Japanese Taste. — Facts and Theories. — Calls from Drs. Brooks and McVickar. — Packing in Wet Weather. — Farewell Presents. — Graduating Exercises. — Near View of the Empress. — Correcting Proof under Difficulties.

Tōkyō, June 29, 1889.

The trouble about the school-building is at last ended, and our school is to have its own building after all. So now the work of moving is going on merrily, and we hope to have a fine time on the 18th, when the Empress will come and make us a speech, a thing she has never done but once before in the annals of the school.

I have been much interested in watching the first few weeks of the life of a Japanese baby, and think that in many respects babies here have an easier time than our American infants at that early age. In the first place, the Japanese baby's dress, though not so pretty as ours, is much more sensible in many ways. It consists, at this season, of a thin, loose, cotton undergarment, with no buttons or pins anywhere about it, and a flannel over-garment made exactly like a grown-up kimono, but tied about the waist with a flannel belt; this kimono is not only long enough to cover the feet, but the sleeves completely cover the hands as well, keeping them from scratching the face, and also keeping them out of the mouth. The poor little weak thing does not have to go through the complicated process of dressing which causes our babies such trials and shrieks every day, but the whole costume can be put on in one minute, and the baby never worry a bit over buttons, sleeves, pins, and strings, as one loose string tied around the waist is all the fastening required. I am sure that if I had a weakly baby to care for, I should put it into Japanese clothes for the sake of saving the daily physical fatigue and nervous strain of our manner of dressing it.

But the dress is not the only thing I admire in the manner of treating Japanese babies. Here, nobody ever makes a noise at a baby, or jiggles or shakes it, to stop its crying. If it cries and cannot be stopped by quiet and gentle means, it is not yelled at or trotted, but just goes on crying until it stops of its own accord, which it pretty soon does. Though my close observation extends to only one baby, I believe from what I have seen outside that this is true in regard to Japanese babies in general. When they grow a little older, they are fully as bright and active and wide-awake as our children, so I do not think that the quiet in which they are kept at first has any effect except to make them less nervous and irritable than American babies.

July 8.

All good Americans celebrated the Fourth by going to the American Minister's ball. I went with the others from a sense of duty, but hardly find myself in my element when I am in a ball-room.

Miné and I have spent a good deal of our time lately in shopping, and find the stores very attractive just now. This is the time of year when presents are given as at New Year's, and consequently the stores are as gay with summer things as they were in December with winter attractions. There is a great festival that begins on the 10th of this month and lasts for three days, when all the spirits of the dead are supposed to come back and walk the earth, and on those three days presents are exchanged. The printed cottons in the stores now are lovely, and I feel tempted to spend all my money in their purchase, for they would be extremely pretty for decorative purposes at home, even where the patterns are too large and queer for our style of dress. I cannot see exactly why the Japanese keep on making the cheapest things so pretty, for many of them are never chosen at all for their beauty, but simply considered for their quality. For instance, there is a kind of blue and white cotton toweling, very coarse, that comes at from one to five cents a yard, that is used by all the coolies and jinrikisha men, and never regarded as pretty or decorative in any way; but still it comes in the loveliest designs, and when freed from its associations with coolies might be used for almost any purpose of house decoration. Now the question that occurs to my mind is this: Why do the manufacturers keep on making these towels in such a beautiful variety of designs, when the purchasers care not at all whether the towels are pretty or not? I have puzzled over this a good deal, and the only answer I can find is this: The instinct of beauty is so strong in the Japanese artisan that things come from his hands beautiful, whether he makes anything pecuniarily by it or not. He cannot help decorating, even when no one notices or cares for his work. It is the same way with the earthenware; everything, from the coarsest and cheapest up to the finest and most delicate, is decorated in some way, and the china stores which contain nothing but the cheapest earthenware used by the commonest of the people are one blaze of beauty in color, form, and decoration. I cannot get at the bottom of the whole thing, or find out how much this instinct of beauty is the cause, and how much the effect, of the gentleness and attractiveness of the common people here, but certain it is, that in this country there is no need of the various missions (flower missions and the like) which have been started in England and America to cultivate the æsthetic sense of the poor in the great cities; for here every poor man's table service is dainty and delicate in the highest degree; even the towel he wipes his face on is pretty enough for an afternoon-tea cloth; his clothes are graceful, artistic, and comfortable; though on a smaller scale, his house is hardly more simple in furnishings, woodwork, etc., than that of the daimiō himself, and as he sits at his work he usually has somewhere about the room a vase of beautifully arranged flowers. One of our workmen would starve on what supports him and his family, and yet the Japanese laborer has his æsthetic nature fully developed, and its gratification within his reach at all times. With him "the life is more than meat," it is beauty as well, and this love of beauty has upon him such a civilizing effect that some people are led to think that the lower classes in Japan do not need Christianity. But when one comes to study them, they are not more moral than our lower classes; they are not as moral; they are only more gentle, more contented, more civilized I should say, except that the word "civilization" is so difficult to define and to understand, that I do not know what it means now as well as I did when I left home.

But this rambling disquisition on the lower classes of Japan grew out of my researches among the blue towels, and may not be as interesting to you to read as it has been to me to write, for I have just been clarifying my own thoughts by writing them down, and you will get, not the finished thought, but simply the boiling over of the kettle in the process of cooking. I suppose that is really all that letters can be, and I am painfully conscious that my letters have had very much of that character on account of my habit of generalizing from a few facts. Please do not believe all my theories, though I think you can trust my facts, for I have never written you anything of that kind that I did not know either at first hand or on good authority. My theories are, I believe, distinctly labeled as theories.

July 17.

My days this week have been enlivened by calls from Dr. Phillips Brooks and Dr. McVickar, who are over here for the summer, and brought me a letter of introduction. At their first call they stayed only a few minutes, so few that I had not time to collect my wits and think of anything interesting to invite them to, for it took me a good part of their call to get over the fear lest they should bump their heads against the ceiling. After living for a year among Japanese, all foreign men seem enormous to me, so you may imagine the effect of those two particularly large men in my little parlor with its low doorway. After they were gone I thought of Mito Yashiki, and obtained permission from the War Department to invite them to go there, sending a note to their lodgings the next morning. Unfortunately, they were out, and I received no answer from them all day. At last, in the evening, as Miné and I were sitting in my parlor, both in Japanese dress,— for I often wear it these warm evenings, it is so comfortable and restful,— we were startled by a cry of " O Kyaku Sama " (" Honorable guests ") from O Kaio as she hurried to open the front door, and there were the two reverend gentlemen, come to bring their answer in person. In this part of the world an evening call is most unusual, so that it was a pleasant and American excitement to have them walk in on us just

ACQUAINTANCES IN TŌKYŌ. 231

as if we were all in America. They could not go with us to the Mito gardens, as they had already filled their time in the city with engagements, but their visit was delightful, for they are the first foreigners I have met since I came to Tōkyō whom I associate in any way with my American life and belongings. It is rather a curious experience for me out here, that in my associations with those about me I am "neither fish, flesh, fowl, nor good red herring." I am too Japanese for the foreigners, and too foreign for the Japanese, too worldly for the missionaries, and not worldly enough for the rest of the foreign colony; and so, with the exception of my intimate Japanese friends, there is no one in Tōkyō who does not seem to regard me as rather out of their line. In many ways I have found Mr. Knapp among the most congenial of my American acquaintances, although my ideas differ widely from his on many subjects.

July 21.

The weather here in Japan is an important factor in one's packing, particularly when the things are to be stored all summer in this damp climate. If the day is rainy everything is damp, and if the things are packed away damp they mould and spot, so in packing one must have sunshiny weather to do it successfully. As yesterday was not bright enough for me to do much, and to-day it is pouring, I am likely to get into quite a hurry when it finally clears, as I hope it will soon.

The children forming one of my classes at school have just been in to bid me goodby and bring me some farewell presents. They are two dolls, representations of the Emperor and Empress, such as are used at the feast of dolls, and various doll furnishings, musical instruments, ceremonial tea-set, bureau, lunch-boxes, etc. A few days ago, another class gave me a beautiful doll dressed in the full costume of a little girl of twelve. The girls had heard me say that I was very much interested in Japanese toys, and had tried to find me pretty ones to take home with me.

Our graduating exercises took place on Thursday, and my special part of the performance, an English speech by one of the graduating class, was regarded as quite a credit to the English department. We were summoned to school at eight o'clock, but as the Empress did not leave the palace until nine, we had some time to wait before anything could begin. At last we were all sent out into the front yard and arranged in line, and we were hardly settled in our places when the imperial carriage drove up, and over we all went in our deepest bow until her Majesty was safely in the house. Then we went in, and word was sent that the Empress would receive the teachers at once, so we hurried upstairs and stood in line outside the door in the order of our rank, until our turns came to go in, make our three bows, and back out again. I had hoped to do better with my bows than the first time I was presented, but as I did not know whereabouts in the room the Empress was sitting, and as it would not have been polite for me to look for myself like a reasonable being, I found myself bowing gravely to the wall, and should have continued to waste my reverence upon that unresponsive object, had I not been rescued from my absurd position by one of her Majesty's chamberlains, who waved me about until I faced in the right direction. When this ordeal was over, we went into the assembly-room, and after the audience was seated word was sent to the Empress, and she came out from her private room. As she reached the door, a chord was struck on the piano, and we all rose; a second chord, and we bowed and remained with heads down until the Empress had walked the whole length of the room, mounted the platform, and spoken the few words by which she formally opened the new building. Then she took her seat in the great black and gold lacquered chair that stood on the dais, the piano sounded again, and we raised our heads once more and took our seats. After this the President of the school came forward, and with many bows and much sucking in of the breath made a speech, in which he thanked the Empress in behalf of the school and its officers. Another of the school's officers followed him with a longer speech, the drift of which I have not yet discovered. Then came the giving of the diplomas, which were not at all like the sheepskins of our native land, but dainty little Japanese scrolls on rollers, with brown and gold brocade mountings. Each girl of the graduating class received hers in person from the President, and had to rise in her place, walk out directly in front of the Empress and bow to her, go to the President and bow to him, receive her roll and bow again, then go sideways until she was in front of the Empress again, bow once more, and back down to her seat. All this bowing had been carefully practiced beforehand, so the girls did it very well and made no mistakes. In the Japanese schools, every pupil promoted into a higher class receives a certificate to that effect, and these are all given by the President at the closing exercises. The classes did not go up to receive these certificates, but the head girl of each class took them from the President for the whole class. As there are twelve classes in the school, and each of the twelve head girls was obliged to make four bows, even this labor-saving arrangement involved a good deal of bowing before all were through. After the diplomas and certificates had all been given, the members of the graduating class made their little speeches, two in Japanese, one in French, and one in English. From my point of view the English was, of course, the most intelligible, and therefore the most interesting. Then there were more speeches and a distribution of prizes, which involved additional bowing, so that by the time the exercises were over my back fairly ached from sympathy. These exercises were interspersed with music, — singing by the school and piano-playing by the girls. The Court band was stationed out of doors under the window, and played when the Empress came in and when she went out, as well as while the diplomas were being given. The first song sung was the one written for the school by the Empress herself. While this was being sung, the audience stood with bowed heads as if in prayer.

I had a better opportunity to see the Empress than I have ever had before, as she sat within a short distance of me for two hours or more. She was dressed entirely in white, and looked very well, her white bonnet setting off to advantage her jet black hair. Her face is long and thin, her forehead high, and her head finely formed. Her expression is sad, and she looks as if these pomps and ceremonies were rather a bore to her. She seemed to take great interest in all the performances of the pupils, whether musical or literary;

more, I thought, than in the speeches of the heads of the school. Somehow I always feel sorry for her, and I think she would be sorry for herself, if she knew how much more fun it is to be a Yankee school-ma'am than an empress.

After the exercises were over, the Empress went out, accompanied by the obeisances of the audience, and we hurried out to the front door, reaching there just in time to bow to her as she got into her carriage. Then there was a lull in the progress of affairs while the guests looked over the building. At last lunch was announced, and we went upstairs to one of the large recitation-rooms, in which a fine foreign lunch sent from the court was served on the Imperial Household's own private dishes. It was a very good lunch, and the dishes were so pretty that it was a pleasure to eat from them. There was a certain feeling of grandeur, too, in using knives and plates decorated with the Emperor's own private crest, — not the chrysanthemum which stands for the government, but the blossoms and leaves of the kiri-tree, (paullownia imperialis), which is the sign of the imperial family, and is put on the Emperor's private property.

An unpleasant sequel to our graduating exercises was that this morning I was aroused from a sound sleep at half past five to correct the proof of the English speech, which was to be printed with the other speeches. I did as well as I could with my eyes half open, and in the dazed condition of one suddenly awakened, but the proof came back again this noon, with word that the printing-office did not understand my corrections. Upon investigation I found that no one in the office knew a word of English, or the signs used in proof-correcting. So Miné and I went over the whole thing again, then Miné explained the corrections in Japanese to the messenger, who went on his way rejoicing.

Wednesday, July 24.

I sail for Kiōtō on Friday, and feel that my Tōkyō life is ended, for my house will be closed, my things packed away, and I a wanderer on the face of the country until I sail for America in September.

CHAPTER XV.

Hiyéi Zan, July 31, to Numadzu, August 28.

View from Hiyéi Zan. — The Mission Camp. — Last Days in Tōkyō. — Voyage to Kobé. — From Kobé to Hiyéi. — Historical Interest of Hiyéi. — Pleasant Weather and Walks. — A Young Buddhist. — Some Effects of the Summer Camp. — Benkei's Relics. — The "Hiyéi Zan Hornet." — Shopping in Kiōto. — The River at Night. — Illumination of the Mountains. — A Snake Story. — Traveling in Japanese Style. — Start in a Typhoon. — Nagoya. — A Wayside Inn. — Okazaki. — Weak Kurumayas. — An Unpleasant Hotel. — Okitsu. — End of the Journey. — Numadzu. — Children's Visits. — Slow Freight. — Plans for Home.

Hiyéi Zan, July 31, 1889.

HERE I am at last, up on the mountain, in the missionary camp. As I sit in my tent, I see below me a deep valley, or rather ravine, and beyond it tier above tier of mountains, their sides flecked here and there with bits of floating mist. One moment the mist drives in and fills up the valley, and we seem to have pitched our tents on the edge of limitless space, then suddenly the cloud rolls away, and we are once more a part of a mountainous world.

I find that I enjoy very much being once more with people of my own race and language, having some one with whom I can talk over the things in which I am interested, and living in an atmosphere so wholly pure and Christian as that in which I now find myself. These people with whom I am are doing a remarkable work, with great wisdom and a spirit of entire consecration to the service on which they have entered. I am sure that the weeks I spend here will be some of the most interesting and instructive that I have spent in Japan, and I shall always be glad that I have had this opportunity to obtain an insight into the lives and work of our missionaries to this country. The annual mission meeting is going on this week, and by special invitation I am privileged to attend it. It does one's soul good to see the company of earnest, cultivated men and women who meet together every day to discuss the plan of campaign for the coming year, and yet the number seems absurdly small for the work that they have done, and even more inadequate for the work that they are planning to do and that is fairly crying out to be done. The great problem is in regard to workers, and much has to be left undone because there are not missionaries enough now to man the old fields, or to open up new ones.

I shall probably write more of the missionaries and their work later, so now I will go back to Tōkyō, and tell you something about my departure thence. The rain of which I complained in my last letter kept on, until at last I had to pack away all my household goods with the dampness in them, and I confidently expect to find everything spoiled that can spoil, when I open my boxes next autumn.

I left Tōkyō last Friday, attended by my maid, who has thus far proved herself a very desirable traveling companion. The steamer by which I went from Yokohama to Kobé was one of the old ones, quite different from the delightful Omi Maru, by which I made the same trip last year, though belonging to the same company. The cabins were full of fleas, and the deck was loaded with horses. I was the only first cabin passenger, and took my meals with the officers of the ship. The bulwarks were so high that one could see nothing while sitting on the deck, and an awning which shut out the glare of sunshine also shut off whatever breeze the bulwarks did not intercept. However, my voyage of twenty-eight hours was pleasanter than I at first expected it would be, for the captain invited me to sit on the bridge, and from there one was able to see all there was to be seen, and catch all the breeze that could be found.

I reached Kobé at about half past four on Saturday afternoon, hoping to go on to Kiōtō and up the mountain that night, but found that the trip was more of an undertaking than I had anticipated, so decided to spend Sunday in Kobé with friends. My woman went on to Kiōtō that night, and met me on Monday at the station with kurumas. The ride out to the mountain from Kiōtō was a very rough one, over a road much washed by recent rains. Just as I was reaching the end of that stage in my journey, the wheel came off of my kuruma, nearly pitching me out upon a picturesque black buffalo loaded with fagots, that was passing. Fortunately, this accident happened so near the end of the kuruma road that it did not delay us at all. At Yasé, where the road ends, we took kago for the lift up the mountain, reaching the camp a little after noon.

Since I have been here I have done nothing but attend meetings, and see my friends, and enjoy to the utmost the beautiful views that lie spread out before us all the time. I mean pretty soon to take some walks and explore the mountain, which is very interesting historically, as it was formerly covered with flourishing Buddhist monasteries. The monks, however, were so warlike and truculent that Hidéyoshi was finally obliged to drive them out, to establish his power in this part of the country. The monasteries were burned to the ground in the sixteenth century, and the mountain left a wilderness. There are now, however, many monasteries and temples upon it, built since the time of Hidéyoshi upon the old sites, so that Christian missionary and Buddhist monk now dwell side by side upon this ancient stronghold of the Buddhist faith.

August 6.

The weather has been delightful ever since I came, and on days when it is too hot for comfort we have only to think of how much hotter it is down below us, to be perfectly satisfied with our situation. It is always cool enough for a pleasant walk after four o'clock in the afternoon, and the walks here are charming, — shaded wood-paths which formerly led to great temples or monasteries, but which now, after winding about the mountain sides, bring us sometimes to a ruined or decaying temple, but more often to an empty terrace where a temple has once been, of which no trace now remains, except the terrace itself, the stone walls that border the path, and perhaps a few overturned stone Buddhas, lanterns, or moss-grown gravestones. Some few of the temples are still kept up, but they have a forlorn and deserted air, and the priests look lonesome and despondent.

The other day, when we were at mission meeting in the big assembly tent, I noticed a young priest standing outside and looking wistfully in. He made quite a picture in his gauzy black robes against the background of green trees and distant blue mountains, and when he turned away and went disconsolately down the mountain side, I felt sorry for him and his decaying places of worship. That evening I learned that the young priest had come down to see one of the missionaries, to tell him that he had decided to leave the priesthood, and wanted to learn about Christianity.

It seems to me that the summer life of these missionaries all together on this mountain side, where they can talk over their work, compare notes, and exchange experiences, and where they learn to know and understand each other thoroughly, is one source of the success that they meet. Here they are like one great family, and when they go back to their widely separated posts, the warm feeling of brotherhood that exists between them strengthens them individually, and gives them collectively a unity of purpose that adds immensely to the force of the mission as a whole.

This mountain, beside being noted as a former Buddhist stronghold, is famed as a favorite resort of the hero Benkei, the Japanese Samson, and the scene of some of his exploits. They show two little temples not far from our camp, joined together by a veranda, so as to suggest the Japanese yoke, which it is said that Benkei saved in time of danger by carrying off on his shoulders and afterward bringing back to their place. There is a well here named for the hero, and to the top of this mountain he dragged the great bell of Miidera that I saw last summer. It was from this mountain's top, too, that he sent the same bell crashing down through the trees until it rolled, cracked and scratched, into the grounds of the monastery that lies at the eastern base of the mountain. So you see we have not only history, but legend connected with this place, and the old stories, joined with the new work that goes out from here year after year into all southern and eastern Japan, give the mountain an extraordinary interest, to my mind.

Kiōtō, August 18.

I am spending Sunday here with some missionary friends, preparatory to my plunge into pure Japan, with no foreign food and no interpreter. I came down the mountain early Friday morning, and felt as if I were leaving a home when I came away from all the pleasant and friendly people there. On Thursday evening, the amusement committee of the camp published a paper, of which I was made the editor, because I seemed to be about the only person on the mountain who was not spending the vacation in the study of the language, or some other work of preparation for the coming year. The paper came out better than I had expected it would, for the different members of the mission sent in a great many short items, advertisements, jokes, etc., and one or two visitors to the camp who were really taking vacation helped out with longer articles, until we had nearly enough material for a "Sunday Herald," or some other monstrosity in journalism. The whole mission seemed in a mood to be amused, and laughed uproariously at the mildest jokes, so the "Hiyéi Zan Hornet" proved itself quite a success.

Since my arrival in Kiōtō I have been devoting myself to shopping, and as I know that I am taking my last look at Japanese shops for some time anyway, I find the temptation to buy everything I see almost irresistible. I never come back from a shopping excursion with more than enough money to pay my jinrikisha man.

Last night, I went with one of my friends for an evening kuruma ride down to the river, which is one of the sights of Kiōtō at this season. The whole surface of the stream was covered with floating tea-houses, brilliantly lighted, and each tea-house was filled with patrons, either eating and drinking or playing some game, — a jolly company, wide-awake, and trying to cool off after the drowsy heat of these August afternoons. The space between the two bridges in the centre of the city was entirely filled with boats, and from either bridge or bank the sight was very gay. Fireworks set off at intervals from one of the larger tea-houses on the shore gave an additional charm to the scene. From there we went to the street on which are all the theatres of the city. The whole street was crowded with people, and looked like a big matsuri; for beside the theatres with their great painted play-bills, there were smaller shows and booths and shops innumerable, with all sorts of attractive wares most temptingly displayed. I had taken the precaution of leaving my money at home, or I should certainly have spent all that I had left from my morning's shopping in buying some of the pretty things that met the eye at every step.

I found that I had come down from Hiyéi Zan at just the right time to see the annual illumination of the mountains that surround Tōkyō. This can be seen better from the part of the city where I am staying than from any other point. The custom was established many years ago by the Emperor, partly for his own pleasure, and partly, I am told, for the sake of killing or driving off snakes and other noxious vermin from the mountains.

The illuminations are produced by great bonfires on the mountain sides, arranged so as to form colossal Chinese characters, and the effect is wonderful, when on every mountain in the circle a letter of fire blazes out clear and distinct through the darkness, burns for an hour or more, and then dies away. Though the Emperor has moved away from Kiōtō, and the bonfires are no longer a salute to his Majesty, the snakes, foxes, monkeys, etc., still live in the mountains, and the custom of scaring them off by these annual fires has not yet been abandoned.

Speaking of snakes reminds me of an incident of our return from a picnic the other day. When we go on picnics on the mountain, we usually engage half as many kagos as there are people in the party, so that each person can ride half the way and walk half, for the American anatomy cannot endure for any great length of time the cramped position necessary in a kago. It was my turn to walk, and I was walking just behind a kago, when the man in front of me cried out, "Mamushi!" and began striking with his stick at something in the little brook that ran beside the path. It proved to be a snake, one of the few poisonous reptiles of Japan. When he had killed it, he poked it out of the water with his stick, and after taking the precaution to crush its head to a jelly against a stone, he took it up in his fingers, opened its mouth, and by a dexterous motion managed to pull off its skin and take out its insides all at once, leaving nothing at all of the snake but its white flesh, as clean and nice looking as a fish ready to be broiled. He then took the flesh, ran a stick through it, and stuck it up on the top of the kago. I was devoured with curiosity to know what he was going to do with the thing, and at last screwed up the courage to ask him. He said that he was going to use it for medicine,—that it made very good medicine. When I reached home I asked O Kaio about it, and she said yes, that the mamushi was good for colds. That it must be cut up very fine and mixed with sugar, and that it made a powerful medicine. She said that once her father was sick and went to see a doctor, who gave him a mamushi, and told him that if he took that all in a week he would get well. The patient thought that if the mamushi taken in a week would make him well, taken in two days it would make him better, so he took it all in two days. But the medicine was too powerful and affected his hearing, so that he became almost deaf. Then he was frightened and sent for the doctor, and the doctor told him that it was because he had taken the medicine too fast. Apparently, the mamushi is in its effects a good deal like quinine.

Okitsu, August 22.

I have been on my travels ever since I last wrote, and am still on my way to Numadzu, but now expect to reach that place to-morrow morning. I am having a delightful time, and my supply of Japanese has answered every requirement thus far. Since Monday morning, — and it is now Thursday evening, — I have not seen a living being who understands English except Bruce, and though I cannot say that I speak like a native yet, I have gained confidence and readiness in the use of the language, so that I am quite convinced that if I stayed here and did this sort of thing a little more, I should learn the language much faster than I have done. I have found out one thing too, which I have for some time suspected, but which I never have put to the proof before, and that is that I can live pretty well on Japanese food, and that at first-class Japanese hotels, with a good maid to look after me, I can be much more comfortable than when traveling, as I did last summer, with a man cook, foreign supplies, and a whole cooking outfit. O Kaio has proved herself perfect as a traveling companion, and I am altogether delighted with my expedition.

And now, to go from glittering generalities to particulars, I must confess that it was with some dread that I bade farewell to my friends at the Kiōtō railway station on Monday morning, for it was in the midst of a typhoon that had blown our umbrellas inside out, and drenched us to the skin. I had almost made up my mind to buy my ticket through to Numadzu, and give up my projected kuruma ride along the Tokaido. But my desire to see how Japanese I could be was not quite drowned out or blown away by, the typhoon, and the thought that I had written home what I had intended to do, and that my friends would consider me weak-minded if I gave it up, helped me to cling to my first purpose and buy my ticket only to Nagoya, intending to leave there in the afternoon for my long kuruma ride to Numadzu. But on the way to Nagoya the typhoon became so violent that it nearly blew the train off the track, and when we reached the hotel and found it quiet and comfortable, I at once decided to spend the night there and wait for better weather. At Nagoya there is a fine old castle, with two enormous gold carp on the top of it as ornaments, so I sent my maid to the city office with my passport and a card, asking for permission to visit the castle either that afternoon or the next morning. They sent me a permit for the next day, so I spent the afternoon in reading and resting and making arrangements for kurumas. Tuesday, however, proved no better than Monday had been. The typhoon was still raging, but I had no more time to spend in waiting for pleasant weather, so started out. First I visited the castle, and was soaked to the skin in seeing it, for though I had bought a long rubber coat in Nagoya, it leaked all over, the wind turned my umbrella inside out, and then when I was trying to turn it back again, broke the handle off short. Thus I was left with nothing but the thinnest kind of summer clothing, and that wet enough to wring, for a ride of thirty miles in an open kuruma, in a wind so strong that the kuruma hoods could not be kept up at all, when we started. Fortunately, a wetting does not chill one in this climate in summer. Even when, a little later, the wind died down enough to permit the raising of the kuruma top, the rain continued to stream down our faces and penetrate to every corner, in spite of all efforts to keep it out, so that bathing-suits would have been more appropriate for our journey than any other costume.

I had made an effort to secure very strong men for the trip, as it was a long one, and must be taken either in very hot or in very wet weather, for these are the alternatives in Japan in August. The man of whom I engaged the kurumayas assured me that they were strong, and fully equal to making the trip from Nagoya to Numadzu in three days or three and a half. I soon saw, however, that instead of having the strong men I had bargained for, my smooth-spoken friend had supplied me with exceptionally weak ones. They ran in an exhausted way, and stopped as often as possible for food, water, or anything else they could think of. At noon we stopped at an ordinary little wayside inn, but O Kaio found me a clean, comfortable room upstairs, where I took off my wet things, and she dried them, a small spot at a time, over a hibachi. When I put them on again they were quite comfortable, although they had a rough-dried appearance that was far from stylish. We ordered lunch, and I trembled somewhat for the result, remembering the tales of Miss Bird and others about the horrors of food obtained at ordinary Japanese inns. However, instead of horrors, a delicious meal of egg and mushroom soup, eels and rice, daintily served in lacquered and porcelain bowls, made its appearance, and I ate with a vigorous relish, for I had an early breakfast, and lunch was served at about two o'clock. The bill for room, fire, and food for two was eighteen cents, and I am sure that nowhere in America can the same amount of comfort be obtained for less than a dollar. After that meal I dismissed all idea of starvation along my journey, for this was only a little country inn, in an out-of-the-way place, and we had letters from our Nagoya hotel-keeper to all the first-class hotels along our route.

That first night we brought up, all wet and tired, at a large, clean, comfortable hotel in the small city of Okazaki, and now I will give you a somewhat detailed account of our stop there, so that you may know exactly how a first-class Japanese hotel cares for its guests.

When our kurumas stop before the door, we are greeted by the whole staff of the house, some coming out to take our baggage, and others on their knees, bowing their foreheads to the floor, just inside the entrance. This cordial welcome on the part of so many bright-faced, well-dressed persons makes the stop at its beginning almost like a home-coming, and is very comforting to the wet and weary traveler. At the door we take off our shoes, and then are led along spotless, polished corridors, and up steep and shining stairs, to a large, airy room, with fine white mats on the floor, and a piazza running around two sides. On our way to the stairs we pass through the kitchen, which is always in the front of the house, and we can stop if we choose to see the process of getting supper, and assure ourselves that the cooking, like all other parts of the hotel service, is clean and neat.

Our room is at the very back of the house, and is the " best room " of the hotel. In front of it is another room, equally good to my uneducated taste, which we can use if we like, and which I finally decide to sleep in.

Our first business is to open our big traveling baskets and take out our thinnest kimonos, then to array ourselves in these loose and comfortable garments, so that our wet clothes may have a chance to dry before the kitchen fire. Tea is brought and cake, and these have a cheering effect. Pretty soon a smiling maid appears, drops on her knees, bows her head to the ground, and presents us each with a bath-gown, with the information that the honorable bath is ready. My maid convoys me down to the bath-room, which proves to be a very open apartment, one side consisting entirely of glass sliding-doors with no curtains. But O Kaio is equal to the emergency, pins up kimonos over the glass, darkens the room by putting the lamp under a bushel, or somewhere where it will not give light unto all that are in the house, and discreetly keeps guard over the door while I enjoy the refreshment of the hot water. Then I array myself in the bath-robe, which serves the double purpose of a garment and a towel, and go back to my room, to sit around on the floor and rest in my loose, cool garments until supper appears, — eels, fish, two kinds of soup, rice, tea, and pickles, all served in the daintiest manner possible. When this is finished, as we are tired and must start by six the next morning, we order up the beds. Silk futons or thick quilts are brought in, as many as I want, and with these and my own sheets and pillows O Kaio makes up as comfortable a bed as any one need ask for. Her own bed consists of one quilt beneath her, and another to draw over her in case the weather turns cool (which it does not), and a wooden pillow. A large mosquito net of green linen is hung from the four corners of the room, and under this the two beds and their occupants are safe from the ravages of the peculiarly small and active Japanese mosquito. There do not seem to be any fleas in this hotel, so we sleep peacefully until aroused at an early hour the next morning by the opening of the shutters, making a noise so like thunder as to set poor Bruce off into a paroxysm of enraged barking. There is no water in our room, but O Kaio takes me out to a neat little washroom, not quite so open and public as the bath-room of the night before, where there is a plentiful supply of cold water and shining brass hand-basins.

When we are ready for it, breakfast is served, — two kinds of soup, rice, and fish, and as I have brought coffee with me, O Kaio makes me a cup, an addition to my breakfast much more satisfying than the weak tea of the country. Then we set forth on our day's journey, prepared to enjoy whatever may turn up.

The weather has cleared in the night, and it seems as if we ought to make good progress, for the roads are neither dusty nor muddy, and the air is fresh and pleasant after the storm. But we soon find that our "strong" men are much used up by yesterday's work, and at last one gives out altogether, complaining of a pain in his "honorable inside," and we hire a puny-looking man to take his place. This causes more delay, the fact that our new man is both small and weak delays us still further, and at last, about noon, the new man gives out and can travel no further. We stop for lunch at a pleasant hotel, and there I have the remaining Nagoya man informed that unless he can find a good, strong man who can get over the ground faster, I will not pay the extra price promised for extra strong men. As a result of this threat, he engages a quick, muscular fellow, who trots along in the shafts as easily as a pony; but then it becomes evident that the Nagoya man is about used up, and has to stop every moment for repairs of one kind or another. I advise him to let me hire new men for the rest of the trip, but as he wants the pay for the whole trip, he insists that he is "dai jobu," and goes on, although he is evidently quite tired out, and keeps calling to the fresh man to go slower.

We travel on in this way, going more and more slowly every mile, until at last, long after dark, the kurumayas dump us at a dirty little hotel in a little village by the name of Maizaka. Here we find that the good rooms are all taken, and at first the people think they cannot even give us a shelter; but our men are too tired to go any further, and at last O Kaio discovers two rooms upstairs, looking out on the village street, in which we take up our abode. The rooms are hot, also noisy, also full of fleas, but we resign ourselves to the inevitable, and send for our supper, which tastes fairly well, though I do not feel sure of its cleanliness, as the whole hotel seems dirty. We have the beds made up early, as we want a good night's sleep before our early start. We go to bed early, but the village does not, and seems to be having a particularly convivial time directly under our windows. There is much conversation and laughter, together with beating of drums and twanging of samisens, which effectually prevents my getting so much as a cat-nap until after twelve o'clock. When the noises stop, I do manage to sleep, but am awakened at half past four for the day. Our only satisfaction at this place is in the bill, which proves to be only sixty sen for the two of us, whereas the morning before, at the pleasant hotel, it had been one yen. However, I think I would rather " darn the expense," and go to one-yen places, than pass many such nights as that at Maizaka.

NUMADZU, August 27.

I have been here now nearly four days, but must go back and finish the journey before I tell you about my present abode. I left off at Maizaka, from which place we started at early dawn on Thursday, hoping to reach Numadzu that night. However, when we came to Hamamatsu, the place where we should have passed the night had our kurumayas been smart, we discovered that one of the bridges ahead of us had been blown away by the typhoon, so that seemed a good occasion for getting rid of our inefficient man by taking the train as far as Shizuoka. This arrangement seemed agreeable to both our kurumayas, and we parted on the best of terms. Then, after an hour of rest in a delightful hotel, where we ought to have spent the night, we took our train for a two hours' ride to Shizuoka, reaching there about twelve. The hotel was partly in foreign style, and they gave me a foreign dinner, with a table and knives and forks, the first I had seen since leaving Nagoya.

At three o'clock we set off with fresh, fast kurumayas, reaching Okitsu at six. Here we found a comfortable hotel and spent the night. Okitsu is quite a fashionable watering-place, with fine surf-bathing. Prince Haru had been spending the summer at this place, but had just left. Here I found Japanese friends from Tōkyō, who gave me a cordial welcome. It was pleasant to hear some English again after my days of confinement to Japanese, for though I know enough to procure the necessaries of life, there is very little else that I can do with the language.

Friday morning we started early, expecting to reach Numadzu by noon, but the typhoon had carried away another bridge, and we had to go several miles out of our way and then cross the river by boat, a course which delayed us several hours. We did reach Numadzu at last, however, and now I am installed in a small room close to the sea, or rather, close to the little hill-surrounded bay on which the hotel stands. It is a lovely place, with the bluest of water, and the greenest of hills sloping down to it. I am living out of doors, for two sides of my room are taken out entirely during the day, giving me not only a fine view of the water, but of the bathhouse as well, into which the whole population of the hotel enters at least twice a day. The guests of the hotel spend most of their time in the salt water, wearing every description of garment, and frequently no garment at all. As soon as they come up from the beach they take a plunge into the warm bath in the bathhouse close by my room, so that there is a continual splashing there from half past five in the morning until nine or ten at night, and a constant procession by my window of men, women, and children. I am now becoming so used to the noises that I can sleep after they begin in the morning, and can go to sleep in the midst of them at night, but for a day or two I found it rather disturbing.

August 28.

Since yesterday I have moved into pleasanter and more retired rooms upstairs, and am now rejoicing in a chair and table for my writing, instead of having to sit on the floor and write on a tea-tray on my lap, as I have done thus far. It is not so noisy as it was below, and I have a corner where I can dress secure from the public gaze; but I rather miss the procession of bathers, and especially the companies of children who used to stop by my piazza and exchange ideas with me through the medium of a little Japanese and a great many smiles and bows and pats of their dainty little hands. They are so delighted to see me wearing Japanese dress, and sitting on the floor and eating with chopsticks, that they are very friendly and curious. Yesterday, I had a long call from about half a dozen of them. They brought me a paper doll as an offering, and came in and sat down on the floor in a semicircle around me. They discovered, by patting and poking and feeling of me, that my hands and my face and my hair were soft, and thereupon there arose a polite contention among them as to who should sit next me and hold my hands, and who should pat my hair, and who should put her face close to mine and rub it gently back and forth. Then they tried, by speaking very slowly and distinctly, to make me understand their Japanese, and were greatly delighted when I did. Japanese children are very attractive and pretty, and they are so gentle and polite that one does not get tired of them as one does of American children.

I am here now without any baggage beyond what I could carry with me in a kuruma, for though I sent my large basket on from Kyōtō by express, and expected to find it waiting for me here, it has not yet arrived, and I am growing daily more destitute in the matter of clothes. I wear Japanese dress all the time in the house, but find it very inconvenient for walking, so have to go out of doors in a rather mussed-looking white dress, not at all the thing for the damp, rainy weather we are having. There is no laundry nearer than Yokohama, so I cannot have anything done up except such articles of clothing as need neither starch nor iron.

I think I must close now. This will be my last letter. My plans for the rest of my time are to leave here on Saturday or Monday for Tōkyō, and to stay there wherever I can find an abiding place, doing up the last things before I leave the country. If all goes well, I hope to reach San Francisco by October 1, and so good-by until some day I sail in at the Golden Gate and bid you all good-morning.

www.ingramcontent.com/pod-product-compliance
Lightning Source LLC
Chambersburg PA
CBHW032102220426
43664CB00008B/1103